A REASON
TO TEACH

A REASON TO TEACH

*Creating Classrooms of
Dignity and Hope*

JAMES A. BEANE

the power of the democratic way

HEINEMANN
Portsmouth, NH

Heinemann
361 Hanover Street
Portsmouth, NH 03801–3912
www.heinemann.com

Offices and agents throughout the world

The author and publisher wish to thank those who have generously given permission to reprint borrowed material:

Figures 2–2 and 2–3 from *Curriculum Integration* by Jim Beane. Copyright © 1997 by Jim Beane. Reprinted by permission of Teachers College Press.

"Spectacular Things Happen Along the Way" by Brian Schultz. Copyright © 2005 by Brian Schultz. Reprinted by permission of the author.

Library of Congress Cataloging-in-Publication Data
Beane, James A., 1944–
   A reason to teach : creating classrooms of dignity and hope / James A. Beane.
     p. cm.
   Includes bibliographical references and index.
   ISBN 0-325-00834-5 (alk. paper)
   1. Democracy—Study and teaching—United States.   2. Education—Aims and objectives—United States.   3. Classroom environment—United States.
I. Title.
LC1091.B38 2005
370.11'5—dc22   2005009949

Editor: Harvey Daniels
Production: Lynne Costa
Cover design: Jenny Jensen Greenleaf
Cover photographs: (left) © Corbis; (center) © Debbra Bohne; (right) © Getty
   Images 24255
Typesetter: Kim Arney
Manufacturing: Jamie Carter

Printed in the United States of America on acid-free paper
T & C Digital 2009

For

Gabriel, Cambria, and Hannah

$\mathscr{C}$ontents

Acknowledgments

Putting together the acknowledgments for a book is a time for celebration. For one thing, it means the writing is almost finished. For another, it means a chance to remember people who have had a hand in shaping the ideas and words involved. This will likely be the last book I try to write from scratch, so over the past several months, I have been thinking about a lot of people who have helped me along the way.

All the time, now, I think about the teachers, staff, and students at Sherman Middle School in Madison, Wisconsin. They let me into their lives the past few years, welcomed me as a colleague, taught me more than they know, and even invited me to teach with them. I especially think about their wonderful principal, Ann Yehle, who keeps the ship on course with her personal courage and commitment to young people. Being treated as a colleague by folks in a school is as good as it gets for a professor. Lucky me.

I have been thinking about my parents, Kay and Jack Beane, a lot. They really believed that schools are important places for children and for the larger society. And they worked hard to make the schools we attended good places for Dick and me. Imagine that.

I have been thinking about the wonderful teachers and colleagues who taught me almost everything I know. When I think about teachers, the first person who comes to mind is always Connie Toepfer. He is my mentor, major professor, and good friend. Talk about luck.

Then there are all the wonderful colleagues and teachers who guided me along: Bob Lux, Sam Alessi, Dick Lipka, Peggy Burke, Phil Eberl, Nancy Scherr, Nancy Doda, Jan Phlegar, Pat Sullivan, Bruce King, Gordon Vars, Mike Apple, Sue Thompson, Dave Braun y Harycki, Trudy Knowles, Mary Klehr, Judy Peppard, Jim Ladwig, and Richard Powell. And then there's Ethel Migra, who shaped the graduate program I describe in Chapter 4 and showed me the far edge of progressive teaching. The luck kept adding up.

Early in my career, I made a decision to work with teachers and to stay closer to schools than the rarefied world of academia. Now I have the luxury of thinking about all the great teachers I met in various IDS cohorts, in the MPEG and NFIC groups, and at the schools where I got a chance to work: Paul Tapogna, Alan Cross, Jeff Maas, Pat Wood, Carol Smith, Ken Bergstrom, Kathy McAvoy, Mark Springer, Dennis Carr, Wally Alexander, Gert Nesin, and so many more. I hope they like this book. I hope it speaks for them, too.

I haven't been able to stop thinking about my university colleague, friend, and now editor, Smokey Daniels. I take full responsibility for the content of this book; he tried as hard as he could to push me forward. It means a lot to work with someone who has personally stood for progressive, democratic education and taken great risks to do that. Meeting Smokey was a stroke of luck for me.

But most of all, I think about the family. Jim, Jason, John, Erin, and Carisima are all such great young people and remarkably kind to their elders. So is Lisa Liebergen and her brothers and cousins. The grandchildren, to whom this book is dedicated, bring joy on the one hand and deep concern on the other, for whether they will live in a more just and humane world seems

more and more in question these days. To know all these wonderful young people is more luck than anyone deserves.

I don't know what to say about Barbara Brodhagen. When a person holds you together personally and professionally and gives you hope, there really are no words adequate to say what should be said. If there were, I would say them to Barbara first of all.

Introduction

Why do we become teachers? Because we want to work with young people? Because we want to teach a subject we love? Because we come from a family of teachers? Because we enjoyed our own school days—or disliked them, and want to do something better? Any of these might do for personal reasons. But there is a more compelling reason that looms much larger over our profession: to help our students learn the democratic way of living. That is the most important purpose for schools. As such it is also our most important reason to teach. Unfortunately the usual way of doing things in schools can hardly be called democratic. So it is that creating democratic classrooms requires that we think again about why and how we do things as teachers.

Most books about changing the way things are done in schools have a certain tone to them. Whatever the new or better idea, it is somewhere out on the horizon waiting to be reached. Teachers will eventually get "out there" after they do a certain number of things. This book takes a different approach. As soon as we make a commitment to "teach the democratic way," we are, in a sense, already out there. Using democratic approaches in the classroom, building a democratic culture, and forming democratic professional communities all will take us deeper into the democratic way. But we don't have to do them first before we can see ourselves as democratic teachers. We simply need to begin acting in democratic ways.

That distinction is very important because while this book is intended to encourage teachers to choose the democratic way, it is mostly intended to show how teaching this way is within their reach. For example, all teachers make countless decisions every day about how to organize the curriculum, what knowledge to emphasize, which activities and resources to use, how to evaluate what happens, how to organize their classrooms, how to group their students, and on and on. The central question in this book is this: *When I choose to teach the democratic way, how will these things be done, and who will decide?* How that question is answered by *any* teacher depends on what they believe about the purpose of schools, the role and rights of students, and their obligations as professional educators. Those who teach the democratic way think about those ideas like this:

- Schools in a democratic society ought to have a curriculum that promotes democracy and the democratic way of life.
- Regardless of their age, young people are citizens in a democracy and have a right to have a say in what happens at school.
- The way to "learn" democracy is to live the democratic way.
- Student participation in planning is only part of the democratic way; the form and content of the curriculum must also embody democratic living.
- Democracy needs a curriculum with a social conscience and a focus on significant personal and social issues.
- Knowledge is not simply a cultural decoration; it is an instrument for understanding self and world and for working on social issues.

Making decisions based on beliefs like that can make all the difference in a classroom or school and, I believe, in our communities and society. I am not so naive or romantic as to believe that the schools alone can carry the democratic way of life. But they do have a certain kind of power as the one place that almost all people spend time in. And most people clearly believe that schools have some degree of power to promote ideas. If not, there wouldn't be such huge debates over what and how young people are taught in schools.

I have organized this book to help teachers think about how they might follow the path of teaching the democratic way. The first chapter lays out the reasoning that brings a teacher to make the commitment to do so. Chapter 2 dives right into the question that teachers most frequently ask: What can I do in my classroom? This chapter focuses on the kinds of decisions every teacher makes and provides a mix of examples of democratic teaching that will help get things going. The chapter closes with an extended account by Brian Schultz of how he and his fifth-grade students brought democracy to life as they tried to lobby for the new school their neighborhood had been promised several years earlier.

Chapter 3 remains largely inside the classroom, speaking to ways of building democratic communities and cultures in the classroom. Chapter 4 looks at how democratic teachers view themselves and considers how they might form democratic professional communities with other educators. This is especially important, since those who choose to teach the democratic way often find it hard to go it alone in schools where everyone else is doing things the usual way. In the last part of this chapter, I describe the ups and downs of a graduate program for teachers that is intended to bring democratic ideas to life. If a real story about teaching the democratic way in graduate school doesn't prove it can be done, probably nothing will.

The last two chapters take a slightly different direction. As John Dewey suggested, educational ideas shouldn't sound good only because they are better than something else. For this reason, the first four chapters contain relatively little criticism of non-democratic ways of teaching. In Chapter 5, however, I offer a critique of the present direction that educational policies and school procedures are taking. It was hard to wait so long because there is a lot to say about this topic. In the last chapter, I offer some hope for reclaiming a democratic purpose in schools.

Although teaching the democratic way has fallen out of fashion under current educational policies (such as the ruthless No Child Left Behind Act), we should not lose hope. The quotes displayed throughout the book demonstrate that democratic education has a long tradition—one that tells us that the democratic way will not simply disappear. The current struggle to resist anti-democratic forces is not the first, nor is it likely to be the last. But already there are signs that advocates for the democratic way are on the rise again. Maybe things have to get worse before they get better, but the number of advocacy groups, journal articles, books, and commission reports is certainly a hopeful sign.

As I put the book together, I talked with many teachers about what should be in it and how it should be organized. And during the several days a week I worked inside one middle school over the past few years, I spent time in classrooms with teachers using democratic approaches. In so doing, I remembered and learned many things. Three in particular should be kept in mind while reading this book. The first is this: Teaching the democratic way often brings teachers into conflict with people inside and outside the school who would rather have less instead of more democracy (or none at all). But being in confrontation with undemocratic people or organizations is not a prerequisite for democratic teaching. Would we stop teaching the democratic way if suddenly there was complete social, economic, and cultural justice and equity in our society? Of course not. It is something we do as a way of life, not simply as a reaction to undemocratic forces. And where do we begin? In the everyday life of our classrooms.

The second idea to be kept in mind is that countless teachers already use many of the approaches and concepts I associate with teaching the democratic way: authentic instruction, project- and problem-based learning, service learning, collaborative problem solving, debates about current issues, and various ways of planning with students, to name a few. If we include all of these teachers in the picture of democratic classrooms, the state of things is much more encouraging than we think. Just as important, though, is that these teachers begin to see what they already do in the context of democracy and give it that name. Not only will it broaden their perspective, but it will give them a higher ground to stand on if their methods come under attack. Standing for democracy is more powerful than standing for a teaching method. And criticizing democracy is much more difficult than attacking a teaching method.

The third thing I began to realize is how many teachers are stuck on an incomplete version of their work. How many teachers have we all met who say that they really love and care about children and whose classrooms are full of engaging and positive activities? Countless. But too many do not seem to understand that if we really care about young people, we need to do more than just brighten their school days. We need to help young people think more deeply about the issues facing the world. We need to help them put their expanding knowledge to work toward making a better world—help them participate as democratic citizens right now, not later on when they are adults. And if we truly care about young people, we also need to work against the injustice and inequities that too often plague their lives and crush their hopes. If this book can help those teachers begin to make that move forward toward teaching the democratic way . . . well, that will really be something!

1 Choosing the Democratic Way

I still remember that beautiful fall day when a colleague and I made the first of what would be many visits to the Children's School. We had heard about the place from a teacher who was taking a graduate course at our university. Quite frankly, it was hard to believe her description. Supposedly, the school was governed collaboratively by teachers and students through town meetings. The students ran their own post office and bicycle repair shop and produced their own plays. And the curriculum was designed to engage children in real-life projects. The further we drove into the rural area, the harder her account was to believe. This was not "alternative" or laboratory school country, with affluent parents looking for a "creative" experience for their children. This was one of the poorest and most isolated counties in the state. Poverty was evident at every turn in the road, and school budgets had little room for showcase programs.

The principal greeted us cordially but, being busy, sent us off to wander on our own around the school. Before long, some children were showing us how to "candle" eggs they were incubating as part of a science experiment. In another room, a small group showed us how they were trying to replicate the recipe for a popular soft drink, while another group took observation notes about the working beehive built into a window. In another room, a young teacher and her students were sitting in a circle planning how they would study the community. Further down the hall, another group explained how their independent reading fit into the continuous-progress literacy program. Closer to the office lobby, three students were moving ceiling tiles around as they "wired" the school for the telegraph system they designed. As usual, we had been prepared to ask the teachers lots of questions about the curriculum. By mid-morning, though, we realized that none of them had said anything to us except "hello." Explaining the curriculum had been left up to the children.

During lunch in the multipurpose room, some children told us how they managed the in-school post office and bicycle repair shop. Halfway through the lunch hour, our conversations were interrupted as the children stopped to watch two brief plays written and produced by small groups of their peers. And when we asked some children about the man in the suit who was helping serve food, one said, "He's the superintendent."

In the afternoon, we were invited to observe the weekly town meeting through which the school was governed. Early-grades teachers used classroom meetings to introduce even the youngest children to collaborative governance. Then, starting in grade 3, they participated in the weekly, whole-school meetings. Held in the library, the meetings were led on a rotating basis by a student who was also responsible for preparing an agenda from ideas submitted by children or teachers. On the day we visited, the agenda began with typical school announcements followed by debate over two issues. One involved whether students should be able to wear hats in school, the other the question of what should be done about students not returning floor cushions to their proper place in the library after using them. Both were resolved by a vote to try out agreed-on solutions and see how they worked. To our surprise, though, the vote itself was conducted by a simple show of hands in which each person, whether teacher or student, had an equal vote. This sharing of power and the trying out of solutions was why, one teacher explained, aside from the usual rules against weapons and drugs, there were only three others posted in the lobby of the school. Those were handwritten on cardboard so they could easily be changed or discarded if experience found them unworkable.

When the school day ended, we finally had a chance to sit down with the principal and teachers to begin asking the many questions we had. How did the school get to be the this way? Who came up with these ideas? How long had this been going on? What did parents say? What did the secondary-school teachers think of this? The faculty patiently answered each question and pulled various documents from file drawers to show us. At the same time, we couldn't help but get the feeling that they felt a bit defensive and frustrated at having to explain things that probably should have been obvious to us after spending the day at the school. Later we would learn that a team from the state's department of education had been sent to the school because achievement scores exceeded the expected range for a school of their size and with their percentage of children in poverty. On top of that, school climate data showed an unusually high sense of community among students and nearly unanimous teacher satisfaction with the school. The visiting team, of course, discovered that the unexpected data from the school were the result of the unexpected things that were happening there. But early on, one state official told me, there had been some hint of suspicion that the scores on those measures may have been tampered with. No wonder the teachers seemed defensive.

Over time, we would come to know more details about the school and the people who worked there, and our appreciation grew accordingly. But whenever we visited, we were always confronted by certain questions. Why was a school like this so unusual? What led the administrators and teachers to think about education and school this way? What did they think about as they made curriculum decisions and interacted with children? What would happen if this kind of school was the norm rather than the exception? This much we did know: With its curriculum based on real-life situations and projects, its participatory governance system, and its emphasis on community and egalitarianism, the Children's School was surely a living example of democratic education.

The Democratic Way

Democracy. Is there any single word that can more quickly describe our deepest hopes or more easily rally us around a cause? *Democracy*: that single word that has been used to justify war and demand peace, to explain excessive private profits and call for social and economic justice, to defend the contributions of powerful political lobbies, and insist on a greater voice for "common" people. How can a word that means so much to people be used for such conflicting purposes? Can it be that such a powerful word should be left to mean anything anyone wants it to? And if it can mean everything, does it end up meaning nothing? Or is there some meaning that democracy was supposed to have, some meaning that has become mired in confusion and ambiguity?

These are important questions for those of us who call ourselves educators. Schools in a democratic society are supposed to play a crucial role in sustaining democracy by helping young people learn the democratic way of life. Many of us were led to believe that of all the purposes demanded of schools, this one rises above the rest. But if the meaning of democracy is so slippery and unclear, then what exactly are we supposed to teach? And how are we supposed to know what to teach if all we were taught about democracy is that it involves voting and memorizing the Constitution?

Educators as a whole are not much different from the general population when it comes to having a wide range of beliefs and values. Along that spectrum, though, is a particular group who call themselves "democratic educators." For them, the preceding questions have certain answers. First, there may be many demands placed on educators and schools, but none is so important as their role in promoting the democratic way of life. Second, democracy does not mean just anything. Instead, it has a particular meaning based on long tradition and difficult struggles. If we want to think about teaching the democratic way, then we must begin with the meaning of democracy.

Democracy is an idea about how people might live together. At the core are two related principles: (1) that people have a fundamental right to human

> The cause of democracy is the moral cause of the dignity and the worth of the individual.
> John Dewey, 1946

dignity and (2) that people have a responsibility to care about the common good and the dignity and welfare of others. Each of these, in turn, has its own defining aspects. The personal right to dignity, for example, includes the right to think for oneself, to be fully informed about important issues, to hold beliefs of one's choosing, to have a say in what and how things are done, to pursue personal aspirations and growth, to be free from oppression, and to experience just and equitable treatment. Caring about the common good and the dignity and welfare of others, meanwhile, includes the obligation to collaborate in resolving community problems; to be well informed about social and political topics; to participate in deliberations about governance and social issues; to promote justice and equity; and to act in ways that generally enhance the social, political, and economic life of the larger society.

Just as those two core ideas—personal dignity and the common good—help to define democracy, they are also the source of constant tension in democratic communities. Examples are not hard to come by. Is it right for one or a few members of a community to exploit others for personal economic gain? Should the government be able to withhold information about threats to public safety because citizens might get upset? Should the owners of media have the right to slant the news or leave out stories they don't like? Should legislatures have the right to prohibit the unhealthy behavior of an individual even when that behavior does not cause harm to others?

The fact that conflicts like these are always present in democratic communities also tells us that the democratic way of living is not aimed at some finish line "out there" where all problems are resolved. There are moments, of course, when people nicely integrate their own self-interest and the common good, as when they vote to raise their own taxes to economically support those who are poor or to improve deteriorating schools. But even then, most issues seem never to be fully resolved, and new ones constantly arise.

Clearly, then, democracy is not simply a matter of voting, participating in making decisions, or having a say in governance. It is not just a "process" or a way of doing things. Democracy is also "about" values like justice and equity. Human dignity and the common good are not only part of how democracy happens, but also what it strives for. Letting everyone have a say in some decision is

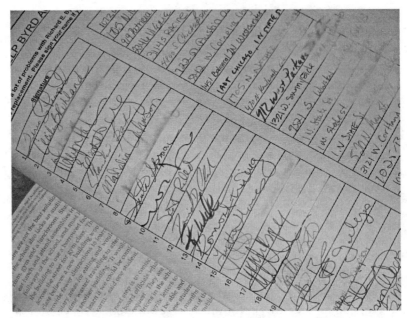

Democracy engages the politics of hope and the language of possibility.

important, but not enough. The decision itself must serve the purposes and values of a democracy and the democratic way of life. It must respect human dignity, honor individual rights, and provide for the common good. This is a tall order indeed. But democracy takes the high moral ground. It engages the politics of hope and speaks the language of human possibility.

The kind of democracy I am describing here is very different from what often passes for democracy in contemporary politics and government. For example, this is not a "naive" democracy that presumes that participation alone is enough to ensure personal dignity and the common good. Nor is it a "private" or merely "self-interested" democracy defined by the often heard statement, "I can do whatever I want. . . . This is a democracy." And it is certainly not the "vulgar" democracy defined as consumers having lots of choices in a free market. Those uses of the term not only diminish the moral dimensions of democracy, but also are frequently used to avoid them. If democracy is only about process, then it does not matter if we act unjustly—only that we talk about it beforehand. If democracy is simply a matter of personal rights, then I have no obligation to work with or help others. And if democracy is only about having marketplace choices, then it does not matter that some of the choices involve harm to the environment or sweatshop labor practices.

If the democracy I am describing is so different from those so-called "democracies," what specific name shall we give it? We could call it "noble" democracy, since it's purposes are dignified and uplifting. Or we could call it "public" democracy, since it is concerned with the common good as much as individual rights. Perhaps we should call it "ethical" or "moral" democracy, since it speaks to deep human values like dignity, compassion, and justice. We could call it "participatory" democracy, as it grows out of collaboration and the right of people to be informed and heard. But we have already seen how it involves more than participation. Some might say it is nothing more than "romantic" democracy, since its faith in human capacity, intelligence and creativity, and generosity toward others seems so hopelessly out of fashion in the cold and harsh rhetoric of today's profit-driven world. Others might counter that it should be called "pure" or "real" democracy, as the call for social and economic justice more clearly reflects the traditions of democratic goals than do obsession with self-interest or marketplace choice. Perhaps, then, we should call it "responsible" democracy, since it does consider the consequences of action beyond profit or self-promotion.

What name shall we give this democracy? How can we make sure that it is not confused with the many others ways that the word is used and abused? Perhaps the answer is to simply call it by its name—democracy. After all, those other versions—the "private," the "vulgar," the merely "process" versions—are not really what democracy was meant to be. They are only clever or uninformed manipulations of the term, and they avoid its larger meaning. And giving the democracy I am describing, a special name would imply that those others are somehow of equal value. It occurs to me, then, that as we explore the idea of democratic teaching, we should have the word *democracy* stand alone, without apology or qualifiers. We should use the word *democracy* as it was meant to be used and so move to reclaim it from manipulation and misuse.

As we explore the possibilities of teaching the democratic way, then, we will want to think of democracy not simply as a form of government where people get to vote, although it is partly that. But at a deeper level, we will want to regard it as a way of being together, of living, learning, and making our lives better. We will think of democracy as an optimistic and humane view of human possibilities, as it proposes that

- all people have an inherent right to dignity;
- we are capable of caring for and about each other;
- we can see our own personal fate tied to that of the common good;
- we have the collective intellectual capacity to resolve the issues we face and the social capacity to work together in doing so.

> *Democracy is America's social faith.*
> George Counts, 1952

This is the kind of democracy we ought to want for our children just as much as we want it for ourselves. And for that reason, it is the kind of democracy we ought to have in mind when we speak of the possibility of democratic schools and classrooms.

Learning the Democratic Way of Life

Sustaining a democratic community depends entirely on the people who are a part of it. Not only do people have to want democracy; they also need to know how to make it work. Knowing how to collaborate with others, how to find and analyze information, how to find and use community resources, how to make plans and decisions, how to communicate ideas, how to take action— all of these and more are necessary skills for participating in and helping to sustain a democratic community. Obviously, we are not born with these kinds of skills or the values and predispositions to act on them. More important, we cannot come by them simply by reading or by being told about them. No, the only way these are learned is through experience: the skills by way of using them and the values and predispositions by seeing how they enrich personal and social life.

What does this mean for the schools and the people who work in them? Quite simply it means transforming the school into a living democratic community. It means asking questions like these:

- How do we think about young people in our school? Are they treated with dignity? Do we talk about them as people or simply as students? Do we speak of our relationship with young people in ways that suggest that school is "us versus them"?
- How does our teaching make use of democratic processes? Do young people have a say in what happens in our classrooms? How do they learn to work together? Are they active and inquiring or simply passive recipients of our words?
- Do the structures of our school treat young people in just and equitable ways? Do all students have access to rich and varied experiences? Do groupings mirror the diversity of the community? Do school outcomes suggest that no group within the school has had a better chance at succeeding than any other? Is there evidence of equitable success among all groups and cultures in the school? Are the resources of the school equitably distributed across the whole school enrollment?
- Does the curriculum include space to learn about and work on personal and social issues inside and outside the school? Does the curriculum respect diverse cultures? Is diversity viewed as a problem to be overcome or as a positive aspect of the school that enriches the possibilities for living and learning?
- Do the adults in the school work as a democratic community? Do they work together on issues and problems? Do they collaborate on curriculum work? Do they reflect on their teaching individually and collaboratively?
- Is the school governed democratically? Do young people, faculty and staff, parents and guardians, and other community members have opportunities to participate in thinking about and making decisions regarding the school?
- Do school staff and policies treat students with dignity and respect? Are communications honest and open? Do all parents and guardians have equitable access to decision-making policies and procedures?

These are not easy questions, but we should not expect them to be. Creating and sustaining democratic communities is hard work.

Yet answers to such questions are not impossible. Democratic education has a long history, and part of that history involves real schools and classrooms

Democracy is not an easy road to take and follow.
John Dewey, 1946

where educators have brought democracy to life. However, just as there is no simple answer to these kinds of questions, there is no single answer. There may be as many different answers as there are classrooms and schools. Democratic communities prize diversity, including diverse ways of doing things. How we actually proceed may depend on any number of things, including where we are located; what grades we teach; how open our colleagues are; what kind of experiences our students have had; and, quite often, how confident we feel. The principles of democracy remain our constant, acting as a compass rather than a detailed road map. The point is to keep moving in their direction.

The questions I have suggested should not be taken as a checklist to be addressed one by one in some order. Creating a democratic school begins wherever we think possible and appropriate. That may mean speaking out against some inequitable practice or structure that benefits some young people while excluding others. Or it may mean beginning in our own classroom with some aspect of our own teaching. Or it may mean opening up a study group with some colleagues. We may decide where to start by thinking about our own classrooms or from hearing about some idea. Or we may begin to act without much thought because we are concerned or even outraged by some school practice or policy that is blatantly undemocratic. Aside from the last option, however, we should be careful not to "overthink" where to begin. There is enough complexity and ambiguity in democracy to have us thinking about it forever without ever actually doing anything. And the creation of democratic schools and classrooms has already been left waiting long enough.

Bringing Democracy to Life

Educators who want to bring democracy to life in schools have ideas like those I have described firmly in their minds. As they carry on the routine details of everyday life in schools, those ideas consistently guide their decisions. Sometimes this is a conscious process, where the kinds of questions listed in the previous section are explicitly asked. But among the thousands of decisions teachers make every day, many happen without explicit deliberation, almost unconsciously. Democracy is a way of life, and when it is thought about and lived long enough, it simply becomes "what we are about" and "the way we do things." In that sense, these seemingly instant decisions by democratic educators are not really as "quick" or "easy" as they seem. All of their experiences and commitments go into them.

Regardless of how long deliberations take, the decisions that result make all the difference in bringing democracy to life in schools and classrooms. What does a democratic school and classroom look like? How do we know when we see one? In a sense, a democratic school is reflected in the details. Thinking seriously about democracy as an idea is crucial, but that idea only has meaning when it shows up in the everyday occurrences of school life—the way decisions are made, the kinds of activities that are emphasized, the way people are grouped, the issues that are given priority, the access to resources, and so on. In short, there are two sides to this coin. Democratic ideas mean little unless we act on them. But methods alone are not enough. There must be intention as well.

> *The values, principles, and processes needed to live effectively the democratic way do not come out of reading texts about them.*
> Gertrude Noar, 1963

I recall some participants at a professional conference eagerly asking if they could visit a teacher who had just explained how her team attempted to create a democratic community and curriculum. They would come for a whole day and looked forward to sitting in on classes. The teacher asked them what they thought they would see. She went on to explain that they might very well be disappointed, because in most ways the team's everyday classrooms looked like a lot of others. Sometimes the teacher and children might be having a discussion. Other times the teacher might be standing up giving directions or presenting information. Still other times the group might be on a field trip or working in small groups on projects. They might be writing in journals or taking a test. The content of a lesson might look just like any other math or science class.

What that teacher was telling those would-be visitors is absolutely crucial for anyone who wants to create a democratic classroom.

It is this. A lot of what democratic educators do is just like what a lot of other teachers do. The methods they use on a regular basis are "good" teaching. What is different are the reasons why they use them and how they are put into place. A lot of teachers use methods like cooperative learning, hands-on projects, portfolios, and group discussions because they are more engaging and experiential than straight lecture and textbook reading. Democratic educators understand that, too, but they are more interested in those kinds of methods because they are part of democratic living. Working together on authentic projects, discussing issues, and keeping an array of evidence about the group's work are the kinds of things that democratic communities do as they work together on issues that concern them.

The teacher was also saying that what the visitors might observe could not be understood as part of a democratic community without considering a larger context. The visitors would probably see cooperative groups, projects, and discussions, and they might say, "We already do that, what's the big deal?" Other things that they observe might come as a surprise: the teacher presenting, giving directions, or working on subject skills of one kind or another. What would the visitors think about this? Would they say, "What a disappointment, that's not democratic"? Perhaps if they had been there at the beginning of the year, when the children and teachers planned the curriculum together, they might see how the activities or methods came to be used. Or maybe on a Friday afternoon, they might get to see small groups of teachers and children reflecting on the week's work and going over plans for next week. Or maybe if they happened to catch a meeting of the steering committee of teachers and students overseeing the present unit, they might get a sense of the classroom's governance structure. Yes, they could see the class constitution on the wall, but they would have to corner someone to find out how it got there. In other words, what the visitors might observe could only be fully understood by knowing the purpose the teachers and students had in mind, the context in which certain methods are used, and the flow of classroom life over time. These things cannot necessarily be "seen" on a visitation day.

Teaching the democratic way means both thinking and acting democratically. The two go together and mean little apart from each other. At times, the thinking part is visible and explicit; at other

times, it seems hidden or almost uncon-
scious. Activity in democratic classrooms can at times be very exciting to
observe; at other times, it can be pretty
mundane. The same can be said of democratic activity in almost any arena, from
community groups to legislatures. What
matters in democratic classrooms is that
teachers and students have a mutual
understanding of democracy as an idea

*Surely it is an obligation of
education in a democracy to
empower the young to
become members of the
public, to participate, and
play articulate roles
in the public space.*
Maxine Greene, 1985

and a sense of satisfaction that the everyday life of the classroom
fits that understanding as much as possible. In that moment,
democracy really does come to life in the school.

What choice shall we make as educators? Shall we continue
to think of schools in ways that have become so common within
much of our profession and in so much of the larger society? Is
the school simply a path to personal ambitions? Is it just an
instrument in the corporate wars of global economic competition? Is it simply preparation for college or a job? Or is there a
much larger and compelling purpose for our schools? Many educators think so. They include the teachers and administrators like
the ones we visited at the Children's School as well as in other
places, large and small, affluent and poor, urban, suburban, and
rural. They hold the values of democracy dear and work hard to
make the school a democratic place. They understand that if we
truly want democracy, then we must choose to teach the democratic way.

2 Teaching for Democracy's Sake

We teachers are constantly concerned about what might be called "technical matters"—the nitty-gritty of classroom organization, learning activities, lesson plans, and so on. And who can blame us? When the bell rings, the time for speculation is over. Something has to happen. And that something needs direction and organization. Certainly, spontaneous moments occur in classrooms, but only someone completely out of touch with classroom life could think that teachers do not have to plan ahead about a wide range of technical details. What are my students supposed to be learning about? What kinds of resources do I need? What activities could we use? How will particular students react to one or another activity?

Moreover, teachers have reasons for the choices they make. Maybe a certain book looks like it will be interesting. Maybe one activity seems like it will be more engaging than another. Perhaps one way of forming small groups would make them more heterogeneous than another way. Whether it is to make the classroom more exciting or more efficient or more equitable or something else, teachers have reasons for what they choose to do in their classrooms.

What happens if a teacher chooses to teach the democratic way? The philosophical commitment described in Chapter 1 is just the start. What happens when the bell rings? When a teacher wants to teach the democratic way, how does that teacher think about what to actually do in the classroom? These are extremely important questions, because while philosophical discussions may avoid them, once the classroom door closes, they demand full attention. And it is in this moment that the most noble intentions of a teacher may come to a screeching halt.

In this chapter, we will consider some of the possibilities for thinking about how to bring democracy to life in the classroom. The intention here is not to write a complete methods guide or recipe, but to imagine how we might think about what to do. After all, there is no one way to bring democracy to life in a classroom, and factors like local circumstances, teacher confidence and security, and the prior experiences of students have to be taken into account. But there are lots of ideas and examples we might draw on to see the connection between classroom details and the democratic way.

Deciding the Democratic Way

In a democracy, the principle of human dignity insists that people have a say in decisions that affect them and that their say counts for something. For this reason, probably no idea is more widely associated with democratic classrooms than the involvement of young people in making decisions about what and how things are done (Boomer et al. 1992).

The portrait of a democratic community is often that of a group of people in careful deliberation, making decisions together about which issues to take on and how to go about the work of the group. Inspiring as that image may be, it implies a kind of open-ended agenda that is not always available in classrooms. Perhaps the implication of that vision is why so many teachers say

> The content needed to teach freedom must include understanding of such great principles of democracy as the worth and integrity of every human being and the right to share in policy making.
> Gertrude Noar, 1963

they can't have a democratic classroom. They may feel that there are too many external mandates to allow an open agenda or that young people don't know enough about what is in a course or subject to make decisions about it. In some cases, teachers even begin to feel guilty because they believe that it is unlikely they can ever reach that idealized portrait.

The fact of the matter is that most teachers do not have the luxury of a completely open agenda. They are hired to teach a particular subject or course whose content and resources have often been decided on by some school or district curriculum committee that is in turn responding to pressure from state standards and assessments. And even where there is a good deal of flexibility, teachers often already have favorite themes or topics they like to bring to the classroom, sometimes having refined them over years of use. In either case, they cannot imagine how young people can be involved in planning.

Instead of beginning with the idealized picture or the real and imagined reasons why young people cannot collaborate in making decisions, perhaps we could begin by thinking about areas in which virtually all teachers make classroom curriculum decisions: the selection of activities and resources, the identification of organizing centers for the curriculum, or the ways in which a group's experience might be evaluated. Within each one of these areas, many decisions have to be made. In a democratic classroom, one of the key questions is, Who will decide about such matters? Will the teacher decide? Will the students decide? Or will the teacher and students decide together?

Suppose it's time to start a yearly unit on cultures, in which students are to read books and poems by authors from diverse cultures as preselected by a curriculum committee. There is nothing here preventing the teacher from asking this year's students, "What questions do you have about cultures?" and then using those questions to guide their discussions about the readings or to expand the unit into new topics. Nor is there anything preventing a high school algebra teacher with a predetermined course, content, and textbook from inviting students to suggest how small groups might be used, how evaluation might be handled, or how homework might be scheduled. Certainly in the case of the high school algebra class, students would have had enough experience in school to know about these things and to have some idea about how they might be arranged.

Many teachers use guided approaches like these, especially one known as K-W-L, originally suggested by Donna Ogle (1986). In this case, students are invited to think about a theme or topic by asking three question: What do we *know* about this? What do we *want* to know? and, later, What did we *learn* and do we still need to learn? In addition to providing an opportunity for student voice and reflection, this and similar approaches help students understand what the theme or topic is about. Jeff Mass, a grade 2–3 teacher, offers an excellent example of how this might happen in Figure 2–1.

In some cases, teachers do have a large degree of discretion in determining the curriculum. For example, Lin Frederick (Nelson with Frederick 1994) and her first-grade students planned their curriculum together through three interrelated steps:

> *A democratic society requires citizens who are skilled in the decision-making process.*
> National Association for Core Curriculum, 1985

1. selecting the target theme (the focus for developing the curriculum);
2. establishing guiding questions to serve as the scope and sequence of the thematic unit; and
3. designing the classroom activities (p. 71).

In one case, they decided to do a unit on "Whales." Next they identified guiding questions for the theme and categorized them according to the different subjects they usually had in school: language arts, music, art, mathematics, and so on. Finally, the group created activities to answer their guiding questions and again discussed how these connected to various subject areas. As well as being an excellent illustration of collaborative planning, this case also tells us that it is not just for older students. Little kids can have big ideas, too.

In another case where wide discretion was possible, this one in a middle school, Barbara Brodhagen describes how she and her teaching partner began the year from scratch with no definite plan for the curriculum. After a few weeks of community

Figure 2–1

The Planets Unit

Not only was this unit designed to meet particular standards within the elementary science curriculum, it also served as a vehicle to demonstrate a fundamental inquiry process, a process that is fundamental to the building of a classroom community. The process:

- Ask a question.
- Gather data.
- Tell others about your discoveries.

This simple inquiry process plays out in many complicated ways during the school year. It is applied in a variety of classroom situations, from individual reading projects to small-group art projects and all-class environmental science projects. The process is intended to tap children's natural curiosity about the world around them and to make their curiosity an important part of the methodology of the community. Making children's questions the legitimate business of learning is inherently democratic. It brings background knowledge, both cultural and intellectual, into the learning community. It creates an atmosphere of ownership and authenticity in the learning community.

The Unit: For this particular unit on the planets, I first asked the kids, "What sort of things do you know about the planets?" Each one generated a list privately of all the things they knew about Earth, the moon, the sun, and any other planets in our solar system. After generating their list, they were assigned to small groups to share their knowledge with their classmates, looking for commonalities within their knowledge as well as any facts that were unique and interesting. After the small-group work, information was shared with the entire class. Key facts were written on a large sheet of paper at the front of the room. When the planet information was shared, I modeled questions that could be generated from the information. ("Why do you think there are thirteen rings on this planet and none on this one?") The modeling was designed to facilitate the generation of student questions and open up possible avenues of research.

After sharing knowledge, I asked, "What do you want to learn about the planets?" Once again, kids wrote privately, then shared their questions with the same small group of classmates, again looking for similarities and differences. Eventually, a group list of *questions* was composed:

What Do You Want to Know?

- What is the temperature on your planet?
- How many moons does your planet have?
- How long is the day (one rotation) on your planet?
- How long is one year (revolution) on your planet?
- What does your planet look like?
- How big is your planet compared to Earth?
- Does your planet have rings?
- Does your planet have storms?
- How far is your planet from the sun?

Children were then assigned a planet. Their charge was to *gather data* on their planet, the second phase of inquiry. Planet groups were constructed ahead of time and were designed to bring together a diverse mix of abilities, knowledge, and cultural backgrounds. For several weeks, kids read books from the library, explored reference books, and searched the Web for answers to the questions generated by the class. All information was kept in a planet folder.

Once all questions had answers, groups had to design a way to *tell others* about their planet, the third phase of the inquiry process. One group made a mobile of their planet. Three planet posters and three dioramas were created. One group wrote and illustrated a small book. Each group presented their planet to the class, answering all the original questions in their presentation.

Extensions: As with most units within our learning community, knowledge generated by the community is extended

Figure 2–1. *Continued*

into other aspects of learning. The inquiry process is a major component of our learning and is repeated in a myriad of forms, lending continuity to otherwise discontinuous events. The facts and information garnered from the planets unit extended into a project with our K–1 classroom buddies. My students were put in the role of teacher, having to design and implement two lessons about the solar system for a K–1 "student." The planets unit also morphed into the children's next creative writing assignment. Kids had to pretend that they were a space traveler visiting a planet of their choice. Information from the planets unit had to be integrated into the writing assignment.

Figure 2–1. *Continued*

building, they took their students through a process she describes this way:

> We begin by asking the students to do some self-reflection: "We would like you to begin by thinking about yourself. Who are you? What are you like? What are your interests, aspirations? Please make a list of words or phrases you would use if asked to tell about yourself."
>
> Next we raise the first of the two major questions: "Still thinking about yourself and looking at the list you have made, now please list questions or concerns you have about yourself. What questions or concerns do you have about yourself?" After sufficient time for the students to list questions individually, we form small groups of five or six people and ask them to search for shared questions which are recorded on newsprint: "Are there questions or concerns that were expressed by several or all members of your group? If so, what are they? No one is required to show their personal list or to share anything from it unless they choose to do so."
>
> Once the group self questions and concerns are recorded, we turn to the second of the two major questions: "Now we would like you to look outside yourself at the world you live in, from the close parts (family, friends, school, cultures, our community, and so on) to the more distant parts (your state, your nation, the global world). We would like you to think about

that world—both near and far—and list questions or concerns you have about that world. What questions do you have about the world you live in?" Again, after sufficient time to record individual questions and concerns, the students are placed in their small groups and asked to find shared "world" questions and concerns (with the same right to remain silent).

At this point the classroom walls are covered by newsprint sheets filled with questions like these:

Self Questions

How long will I live?

What will I look like when I am older?

Do other people think I am the way I think I am?

What job will I have?

What would I do if I met an extraterrestrial?

Will I ever go to outer space?

Why do I fight with my brother and sister?

Should I get a tattoo?

Will I be poor and homeless?

Will my family still be there when I am older?

Will my parents accept me as an adult?

Where will I live when I am older?

Will I get married and have children?

Why do I act the way I do?

Why do I have to go to school?

Will I have the same friends when I am older?

Why do I look the way I do?

Will I go to college?

Will I be like my parents?

World Questions

Will we ever live in outer space?

What will happen to the earth in the future?

Why are there so many crimes?

Why do people hate each other?

Why are there so many poor people?

Will racism ever end?

Where does garbage go?

Who will win the next election?

Why are schools the way they are?

Will the rain forests be saved?

Why is there so much prejudice?

What is the purpose of time?

How do you know when something is real?

World Questions (*continued*)

Will there ever be a president who is not a white man?

Are there other planets than the ones we know about?

Who owns outer space?

Will the U.S. ever be out of debt?

Will cures be found for cancer and AIDS?

Will drug dealing stop?

What will people evolve to look like?

Will hoverboards replace skateboards?

Is time travel possible?

How many kinds of species are there?

Next we ask the small groups to look at their self and world questions to identify themes for the curriculum: "Are there any cases where there are connections between self and world questions (such as questions about conflict in school and conflict in the larger world)? If so, what are some words or phrases you might use to make connections (such as "conflict")?" (In groups of 60 or less we have also done this by posting all questions from small groups in a central location and asking the large group to find themes.)

Teaching the democratic way means involving students in planning the curriculum.

Next, the lists of themes from the small groups are posted and the large group reaches consensus on a single list. A vote is then taken to select the first theme for the year (with the rest of the themes to be addressed later). Having selected an opening theme, the small groups are reconvened to identify questions and concerns from their lists that they would include within the first theme: "What are specific self and world questions and concerns we might want to answer within this theme? Be sure to indicate which questions are of interest to all or most of the group and which to one or two since there will be room for both large and small group activities." (For this task we have also used a steering committee with a representative from each small group.)

Finally, we ask the students to identify possible activities the group might do and resources they might use to answer the questions for the theme. To do this we use one of several ways: small groups rotating through stations where one or two questions are posted, large group discussion, or dividing the group in half.

This process completed, the teachers proceed to organize and expand the activities, develop a calendar for activities and projects, and so on. The teachers and students also create a web for the unit as a visual organizer.

Among other things, these examples show that there is no one way to involve young people in making classroom curriculum decisions. The point is to continuously ask, How can students be involved? Sometimes the possibilities may be limited; other times they may be wide open. Teaching the democratic way means involving young people in decision making whenever possible and to whatever degree possible. Giving students a voice in this way, no matter how restricted the teacher may feel by various mandates, is a step in the democratic direction.

A word of caution is needed here, however. I have heard many teachers who have done a bit of collaborative planning with students excitedly say something like, "They decided to do just what I would have planned." This should come as no great surprise. Students are real people, too. They live in the world and they have been to school. If we ask them what questions they have about cultures or how to organize small groups or what questions they have about the world, they are very likely to come up with ideas that look like ours. But the word of caution is this: The purpose of involving students in planning is not to trick them into thinking that our ideas are theirs or to subtly lead them to the plan we already had in mind. Tricking students or engineering their consent is not consistent with the democratic way. The purpose of involving students in planning is to help them learn the democratic way. Whether their ideas match ours is not the point.

For some teachers, the possibility of involving students in planning simply sounds like too much work. There is no denying that collaborative planning can be difficult and that it involves more complex skills than merely telling students what to do. On the other hand, too many teachers find themselves in a constant struggle with students because there is no mutual understanding of what is supposed to happen or the teacher has guessed wrong about the best way to do things. Worse yet, many teachers find themselves in long meetings trying to figure out with colleagues what might work with students. Why would teachers think that these struggles, meetings, and moments of bad guesswork are less work, let alone less frustrating, than planning up front with their students about how things might happen in their classrooms? More difficult? Perhaps. More complex? Yes. More work? Not in the long run. Collaborative communities are a lot less work than adversarial ones.

For other teachers, the very idea of planning with students seems almost impossible because it means letting go of their complete control of classroom life. Teachers are certainly entitled to such feelings, since most have probably had little preparation for planning with students, and moreover, they are responsible for what happens in their classroom. At the risk of seeming overly harsh, though, I want to ask the question, Whose education are we talking about here? In a democratic society, public participation in making decisions does not depend on whether elected officials feel comfortable with the idea. It is about the rights and responsibilities of citizens and the obligations of elected officials. Likewise in the classroom, the matter of collaborative planning is not really about the feelings of the teacher. True, the teacher must make many decisions alone regarding the safety and well-being of students. But there are still countless matters open to consideration in a classroom. In these matters, collab-

> *Students who are able to participate in making decisions at school are more committed to decision making and democracy in other contexts.*
> Alfie Kohn, 1996

orative planning is about the right and responsibility of young people to learn the democratic way and the obligation of the teacher to help them do so.

So how can a teacher get started in planning with students? First, set aside any feelings of guilt over how little or much seems possible. Second, be honest with students. Tell them what you plan to do and why, and how you hope it will happen. Third, select a way that seems doable.

- Try asking students what questions they have about a theme you feel knowledgeable about.
- Ask them what kinds of activities they have had good experiences with in the past, and use the information to plan activities for an upcoming unit.
- Bring a unit plan you already have to your students. Ask them to look it over and give you suggestions.
- As part of getting to know your students, ask them what questions they have about themselves and the world. Collect these and think about how they might be incorporated into units you plan to do. Or study the questions to identify themes you might use during the year.

Obviously, there are lots of ways to involve students in planning. The way to get started is to pick one and try it out. If it doesn't work, try another. Remember, most young people have never been asked to be involved in classroom planning, so they may be as apprehensive as we are. The first request for their ideas may be met with silence or a remark like, "You're the teacher, you decide." But over time, we can help them find their way just as we will find ours. And that search, in and of itself, is an important part of the democratic way.

Notice, though, that in all of the examples of collaborative planning I cited, none involved simply asking students, "What do you want to do?" or "What are you interested in?" As we will see in the next section, teaching the democratic way is not a matter of whimsical ideas or of doing whatever we are interested in. Democratic communities take on particular kinds of issues and concerns. People may find them interesting and enjoy working on them. But even if they don't, the issues and concerns of democracy must still be addressed.

Content Worth Teaching

In the first chapter, I tried to emphasize that democracy is not simply a process. It is about something. In the same way, democratic classrooms are defined not only by how things are done, but also by the topics, issues, and questions they focus on. Like all teachers, those who choose to teach the democratic way are faced with a myriad of expectations about the content and skills they are supposed to cover. But they constantly seek ways to make space for socially significant topics and themes by explicitly using them to organize the curriculum or by working them into the subjects they are mandated to teach. In so doing, they think about knowledge as more than just cultural ornamentation and more than a collection of facts or skills that their students must have to get through a test or on to the next grade. For these teachers, knowledge is an instrument for understanding and resolving socially significant topics and problems.

> Democratizing curriculum and education means, in its broadest sense, connecting learning in the classroom with the use of knowledge in settings near and far.
> Ed Mikel, 2000

Here, as in the case of collaborative planning, there may be a wide range of possibilities, depending on the experience of the teacher and the amount of discretionary space in the curriculum. In search of content for math problems, teachers and textbook authors seem most often to turn to simple situations, such as dividing up food among friends, making change from multiple purchases, or finding distances around an imaginary town. Teachers who are thinking about the democratic way are more likely to search for examples having to do with more significant topics, such as trends in local population patterns, distribution of wealth, or effects of different land-use patterns. Where lists of preferred stories and poetry often emphasize classical "musts" or "child favorites," teachers who choose the democratic way are also on the lookout for those that bring to light important contemporary issues and that systematically give voice to views from diverse cultures.

Topics and problems in science are not simply drawn from simulations or exercises in a manual when teachers are thinking about democracy. Instead, they are more likely to involve things such as testing water in the school or community, analyzing the nutritional value and consequences of cafeteria food, identifying pollution sources in the local area, and studying and debating trends in scientific and medical research and funding. Social studies is not merely a chronology of events defined by wars and land acquisition deals populated by military figures and politicians. It is a study of recurring issues and problems like human rights, civil liberties, and economic justice that are struggled over by real people from diverse backgrounds who influence and are influenced by social, political, and cultural forces (Lockwood and Harris 1985). Music and art are not simply areas for clever activity, holiday performance, or high culture appreciation, but opportunities to express hopes and feelings in relation to life's events and struggles.

Thinking about such examples reveals some of the kinds of questions teachers can ask when they choose to teach the democratic way:

- Does the content of a particular subject involve socially significant issues and topics whenever possible?
- How can I use my subject to bring to light important issues or topics?
- Are students aware of my attempts to add social value to a subject?

Teachers who have not thought about these kinds of questions might be surprised to find that taking them seriously not only begins to bring democracy to life, but also helps bring mechanical or abstract content and skills to life. This is becoming increasingly important as teachers are mandated to use standards-based, packaged, and scripted curriculum materials that are sanitized of social issues so as not to inhibit sales in any particular state or community. Examples are not hard to find: popular science programs that include a unit on genetics without mentioning how the proportion of a person's blood from different ethnic backgrounds was historically used for racial profiling and discrimination; or math programs that have students calculate family budgets

> *What avail is it to win prescribed amounts of information about geography and history, to win ability to read and write, if in the process the individual loses his soul.*
> John Dewey, 1938

as if every family enjoyed a living wage. Most of these materials may seem like good subject content to the subject specialists who create them, but they are inconsistent with the lived realities of many young people and lacking in any social conscience.

Another way of bringing the content of democracy to the surface is found in classrooms where teachers organize the curriculum around personally and socially significant themes (Beane 1990b, 1997; Daniels and Bizar 1998; Faunce and Bossing 1951). Sometimes identified in collaboration with students and sometimes by the teacher alone, such themes provide opportunities for young people to simultaneously think about themselves and the world around them and to use a variety of content and skills. For example, picture a unit called "Living in the Future" (see Figure 2–2), in which young people do survey research to identify concerns about the future, design inventions to solve environmental problems, examine the accuracy of forecasts that had been made for their own time, and make recommendations to their city planning office for dealing with anticipated future problem areas such as land use, transportation, and housing (Brodhagen, Weilbacher, and Beane 1998). Consider another, entitled "Show Me the Money" (see Figure 2–3), created out of questions young people had about where money came from, how it is distributed, how it is manufactured, how to budget, and how much various occupations pay (Beane, Brodhagen, and Weilbacher 2005). To answer such questions, students engage in a variety of activities, including researching the evolution of barter and money in ancient civilizations; creating budgets for both wealthy and poor families; studying statistical trends on the distribution of wealth; inventing improvements in our economic system; and investigating the economy of countries where their favorite clothes are made, including conditions of sweatshop slavery in those countries. Then imagine the group moving to a new theme entitled "Conflict" that involves questions like: Will there be another world war? Why is there so much prejudice? and Did the Civil War ever end?

Still other teachers prefer to engage young people in a direct approach to democratic living by organizing major portions of the curriculum explicitly around social problems and service learning. Such was the case some years ago when a first-grade teacher in a Midwest school began the year with a field trip to a

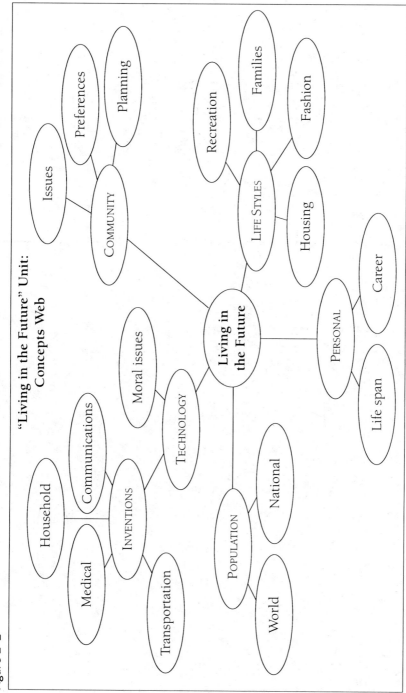

Figure 2–2

"Living in the Future" Unit: Concepts Web

Figure 2–3

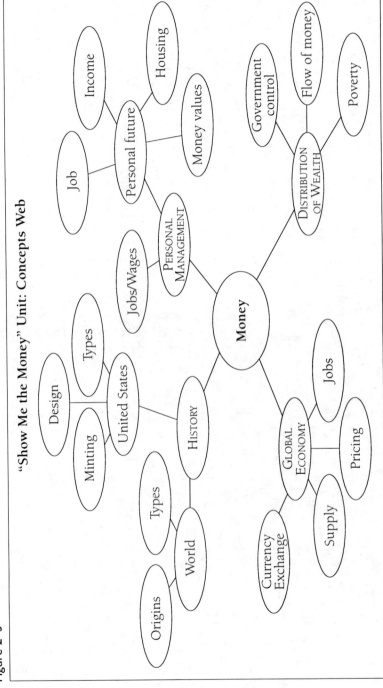

"Show Me the Money" Unit: Concepts Web

local landfill so that the children could see firsthand the effects of unnecessary waste. With that issue in mind, the year was spent creating posters and songs and reading and writing stories about conservation, raising money to plant trees on school grounds, and helping other people in the school learn to recycle. More recently, at a high school in another school district, a teacher and group of students in a computer class used statistical mapping software to show the effects of a grocery store's closing on surrounding neighborhoods. Their data were then used by a neighborhood activist organization to lobby for a new grocery store rather than some other kind of business for that commercial space. In still another example, Grady (2003/2004) describes how students from the Cambridge Rindge and Latin School in Massachusetts used data they gathered from peers to study and make recommendations for addressing public health issues among adolescents. In addition to specific ideas for improving public health, the data also serve as a basis for additional work by new groups of students each year.

Teachers at all levels do these kinds of units or projects, and their stories often appear in newspapers and on television news, especially when the social problems are local. Ironically, though, the reports usually portray these experiences as supplemental to some other course work or as fillers when other work is completed. In some cases that is true. But for many of those teachers, this is the curriculum, for social problems are, after all, the content of democratic work.

In addition to using content of social significance, teaching the democratic way demands that content be drawn from more than the usual academic sources (namely, textbooks) or sources that present only one cultural view. In a democracy, the question Whose knowledge is of most worth? is extremely important. The democratic right to have a voice and the related responsibility to hear many voices require that teachers and students draw content not only from the traditional disciplines of knowledge but also from their own personal knowledge, popular culture, and current media. Moreover, they are obligated to seek ideas and viewpoints of diverse cultures.

I am reminded of a teacher I met who claimed to be working in a community that had no diversity, and for that reason he felt he didn't have to use multicultural resources. Of course, he had confused race with culture, mistakenly believing that since everyone was white, there was only one culture at work in his town. But even if he had been right about that, he was wrong about his obligation to engage students with multicultural views. In fact, the apparent lack of diversity should have inspired him all the more in his search for multicultural resources. The democratic way prizes diversity for the richness and variety of resources and ideas it offers. Critical analysis and debate may end up giving more weight to one view or another, but in a democracy, no one has a monopoly on knowledge and everyone has a right and responsibility to hear diverse views.

I began this section by noting examples of how social issues might be inserted into the content of various subjects. However, many teachers in search of democratic methods have come to the conclusion that teaching the democratic way eventually involves moving beyond the separate-subject approach to curriculum toward approaches that integrate knowledge through problem-centered units (Beane 1997; Nagel 1996). This makes good sense when we understand that no problem of any social significance can be understood or resolved using only one subject. For example, statistics about hunger may help us to understand the scope of this problem. But to really work on the problem of hunger requires getting information about health, doing political analyses of budgets, speaking out at meetings, writing reports, creating artistic displays, and so on. University scholars and scientists understand this, as evidenced by the increasing emphasis on interdisciplinary programs on topics like environmental studies, cultural diversity, and integrated medicine. Knowledge organized for the sake of democracy is not separated into bits and pieces of separate subjects taught as if they had little or nothing to do with one another and memorized for some test. Nor is it drawn only from academic or single-culture sources. Instead, it is pulled together from a variety of sources in an integrated way so that it can be put to use on a significant topic or problem. And in that form it becomes knowledge for the sake of democracy.

> *Thematic investigation thus becomes a common striving towards awareness of reality and towards self awareness.*
> Paulo Freire, 1970

This idea is not just some theory. Santone (2003/2004) describes how the theme of *Sustainability* can include a wide range of problem-centered projects from redeveloping local land to investigating global resource issues. In the book *Democratic Schools,* teachers and administrators from several classrooms and schools describe how they bring democracy to life. In every case, the authors mention using problem-centered thematic units to help organize the curriculum in their classrooms and schools (Apple and Beane 1995). Among the themes cited, which are from all levels of schooling, are justice, city works, making a difference on planet Earth, and racism and prejudice (Meier and Schwartz 1995; Rosenstock and Steinberg 1995). This should not be a surprise. A lot of teachers use themes in this curriculum. The difference here is where the themes come from. Some teachers draw themes from existing subjects such as colonial living or metrics. Or they use "processes" change or cycles. Or they use appealing topics such as dinosaurs or inventions. But for those who want to teach the democratic way, the most important source of themes is significant social issues and topics. A closer look at the themes used to organize the curriculum at one of those schools, La Escuela Fratney/Fratney School (2003/2004), makes this point especially clear:

Theme I: We respect ourselves and our world.

Every living thing has needs.

I am somebody important.

We all have a cultural heritage.

We need to live in peace.

TV can be dangerous to our health.

Theme II: We are proud to be bilingual, multicultural learners.

Diversity is a strength in our society.

There are many benefits to being bilingual.

We communicate in many languages and in many ways.

We learn from and teach each other in our Fratney community.

We recognize and respect our multiple languages, cultures, and experiences.

We learn to counteract the stereotypes contained in cartoons, books, magazines, and the media.

Theme III: We can make a difference on planet Earth.

We have been shaped by the past, we shape the future.

African American people have contributed greatly to our nation.

We celebrate the contributions of women.

People of all nationalities have worked for justice and equality.

We need to overcome prejudice and racism.

Theme IV: We share stories of the world.

My family's story is important.

We learn about other people through their stories.

We can all be storytellers and actors.

Other kinds of themes, taken from other sources, might lend themselves to interesting activities and give some context to various skills or facts. But they do not speak to the problems and concerns that occupy the work of democratic communities. Nor do they help young people learn the democratic way.

Doing Things the Democratic Way

Sometimes people talk about the democratic way of life as if it is only about getting together for planning and decision making. In fact, students who first find themselves involved in planning as part of a democratic classroom have been known to ask, "Are we going to do anything this year or just plan?" But democracy is also about doing things and getting things done. The democratic way of living is an active one as people search for informed opinion, analyze situations, express viewpoints, create solutions, offer recommendations, and take direct action. Teaching the democratic way thus involves active classrooms as well as particular kinds of activities.

In democratic communities, people spend a good deal of time and energy becoming well informed about important issues, topics, and problems. In a democratic classroom, we thus might expect to see young people frequently engaged in researching the questions and concerns they have helped to identify. In an age of communication such as ours, sources of information are increasingly accessible, inside and outside the school, through technology, personal contact, and all kinds of media. Teaching the democratic way means seeking different viewpoints from a variety of sources and helping young people to become increasingly adept as critical consumers of information. In a democratic classroom, teachers and students are interested not only in what is said, but also in who is saying it, why, and by what authority—a scrutiny that may extend from media commercials to textbook authors.

In addition to gathering and critically analyzing information, democracy requires learning how to share it with others. This is why democratic classrooms place a premium on informed discussions and debates as well as presentations and performances. Suppose, for example, the students are considering what they would like their town or city to be like twenty-five years in the future. They might identify important aspects of community life (like land use, transportation, social services, and recreation) and then form small groups around each one to gather information and make recommendations. Rather than stopping there, as might happen in some classrooms, the small-group recommendations would be debated, revised, and voted into an integrated and comprehensive set of recommendations and submitted to town or city authorities.

Because concern for the common good is a hallmark of democratic living, we might also expect to see groups in democratic classrooms involved in various kinds of community service, especially through service learning. According to the National Service Learning Clearinghouse website, service learning "combines service objectives with learning objectives with the intent that the activity change both the recipient and the provider of the service. This is accomplished by combining service tasks with structured opportunities that link the task to self-reflection, self-discovery, and the acquisition and comprehension of values, skills, and knowledge content."

Without demeaning short-term acts of charity or kindness, teaching the democratic way involves looking for ways to engage young people in more

> *Service learning projects not only have a legitimate place in the school program, but they may be initiated from virtually any aspect of it.*
> Richard Lipka, 1997

complex projects by which they may not only experience a sense of altruism but also learn how to act on problems and concerns. Earlier I mentioned two examples, one in which young children pushed for more recycling in their school and another in which older students used mapping software to show the effects of a grocery store closing. Hundreds more examples have been reported over the years, from designing school playgrounds to conducting community surveys to registering voters to organizing public health campaigns. There is no shortage of examples such as these, but there is a need for both educators and the public to recognize such projects not simply as charity but as part of a larger understanding of teaching and learning the democratic way.

Sometimes those kinds of activities are found in classrooms where the intent is to make learning more engaging or hands-on. Used this way, they are often the center of debate about whether they result in high achievement, enough content coverage, or even too much noise. Sometimes they are criticized because they lead young people to demand action on issues in the school or community. And nothing can chill a classroom more than the administrative admonition, "Don't light any fires we can't put out." But where educators are committed to teaching the democratic way, these criticisms are badly misdirected. Aside from the fact that active learning leads to better academic achievement (see, for example, Marks, Newmann, and Gamoran 1996; Newmann and Associates 1996; Thomas 2000), the central purpose of democracy requires particular kinds of activities not because they are clever or engaging or exciting or fun, but because they are the way of doing things in democratic communities.

> With the development of these four, (1) a sense of the personal worth of every human being, (2) the ability to communicate with others, (3) the ability to face and solve problems, (4) self-direction and the ability to work cooperatively with others, comes a fifth and major value, namely, an understanding of the meaning of democracy.
> Rosalind Zapf, 1959

One other premium approach in democratic classrooms needs to be mentioned here for both its importance and the controversy surrounding it: having students work together on projects and other activities. What to call this approach these days is not an easy question. The original name, *cooperative learning*, has fallen somewhat out of fashion because it often came to be associated with academic games more than social learning and because conservative critics thought that it detracted from the individualistic competition they associate with capitalism. For social and political reasons, then, many educators have come to use the term *collaborative learning* instead. Either way, though, it is hard to imagine a democratic community or classroom in which students are not frequently working together. Collaboration and cooperation are icons of democratic life.

Ironically, the use of such groups has fallen into disrepute in many places under the weight of criticisms that they hold back "gifted" children who have to "carry" the group. This sort of reasoning suggests how far our schools have wandered from an understanding of democracy and its role as a central purpose in education. If the purpose of schooling were to teach young people how to compete for personal gain, the critics would surely have a point. But we look to cooperative and collaborative groups not just for their widely documented academic benefits (see, for example, Johnson et al. 1991), but also because they are a critical also aspect of living and learning the democratic way. The dilemmas they pose, such as how to work together and how to deal with those who don't pull their weight, are not reasons to avoid cooperative groups; they are reasons to use them. The response to critics is not so much an argument about achievement as it is a claim for democracy and the obligations of schools in a democratic society. Some years ago, my mother, herself a progressive teacher in the 1930s, expressed surprise that debates over cooperative and heterogeneous groups continued some sixty years after she thought they were settled. Explaining a bit of the current political context, I asked her what she would say to parents who demand to know what their "gifted" children will get out of such groups. Her response was quick: "They learn to lend a hand." Sometimes the obvious answer is the most compelling.

Evaluating the Democratic Way

It is often said that the best way to tell what educators value is to look at what they evaluate. When it comes to teaching the democratic way, however, the question is not only what is evaluated but also how. In thinking about classroom curriculum planning, we recognized the fundamental idea that people have a right to have a say in decisions that affect them. That same idea applies to designing evaluation. One way of getting started with involving students in designing evaluations is to ask them straight out how they think their own work, the curriculum, the groups' efforts, the teacher's role, or anything else might be evaluated. Should we use a scaled survey, a test, a performance, a discussion, a written narrative, a portfolio?

As a prelude to the larger question, the teacher alone—or with students—might create a list of various types of evaluation methods so as to guide the discussion of which to actually use for a particular situation. Is it undemocratic for the teacher to offer a list of possibilities for the students to consider? Of course not—so long as there really is a difference between them and the students' choice or recommendations will be taken seriously. And depending on the situation, the best choice from a democratic viewpoint might be to use several different methods so that different students might find the one that gives them the best opportunity to show their work or ideas.

Students might also be involved in helping to create any given type of evaluation (Brodhagen 1994). For example, before projects or other work is under way, the group might design rubrics for evaluating them, from the content requirements to the quality of exhibits and presentations. The whole group or a committee might look at the comment sections on report cards to see if the language is clear or if additional or different comments should be included. Also, they might design a format for student-led conferences or project performances.

The principle of student voice also applies to answering the question of who evaluates student work. Obviously, teachers must be involved in evaluating and reporting the work of students. Even if they are reluctant to do so, parents and school authorities insist on it as part of the teacher's responsibilities. But teaching and learning the democratic way means that students must also play a crucial role with regard to their own work. Aside from the right to have a say about how they did, young people also deserve and benefit from opportunities to become more skilled in making judgments about their own efforts. Thus, in democratic classrooms, teachers make every effort to engage students in reflection and self-evaluation through discussions, conferences, journals, guided self-evaluation forms, and other means. At the end of units or grading periods, students complete self-evaluation activities that are placed in portfolios and shared with parents or guardians. A high premium is placed on student-led conferences in which self-evaluation results and future goals are discussed with teachers and parents or guardians. And where midterm or final report cards are used, two columns of grades or comments are included— one for the teacher and the other for the student. Here again, though, teaching the democratic way means framing these kinds of activities in terms of the right to participate in evaluation rather than as a clever device for forcing students who have not completed their work to publicly admit it.

> *In our society we grade roads, eggs, and children, and the latter have just as much to say about their grades as the first two.*
> Richard Lipka

When teachers choose to teach the democratic way, they are also concerned about the work of the large group and that of small groups used for special projects. In this case, arrangements are made for reflective evaluation through discussions, structured response forms, and other means. Here crucial questions are asked about how group work integrates the values associated with the democratic way of doing things. Did group members have equitable opportunities to participate and to have their ideas heard? Were decisions made using some process of thoughtful consensus? Were efforts made to encourage everyone to contribute to discussions and decisions? Did materials and other resources considered by the group reflect a range of viewpoints? Did group leaders, including the teacher, encourage the group to be thoughtful and respectful in collaborative work and communications? Were efforts made to have diversity in small groups? Was ample time allotted for planning, conducting, and evaluating individual and group work?

Using the idea of inquiry, students might also study state standards as well as sample or so-called "released" items from state or district content tests. Doing so opens up opportunities to reflect on how their learning experiences have helped them meet external requirements or prepare for various tests. In a time when such mandates are so heavily weighted, students have a right to this kind of information. On the other hand, taking such inquiry to a critical level may also help students begin to see how these testing regimes involve undemocratic political interference in their lives and schools.

Many teachers have never had experience with these kinds of democratic evaluation ideas. Here are some ways they might get started.

- Create a form for students to answer questions about how they did on a project.
- Ask students to write a short self-evaluation statement to bring home at midterm, and indicate whether you agree or disagree with the statement.
- Invite students to submit questions for a content test—and then use them.
- Set aside some time at the end of the day or period on Friday to discuss how things went during the week, and again on Monday to preview the new week's plans.
- Ask a small group of students to come up with a rubric for assessing aspects of a project.

And remember, most young people have probably never been asked to participate in evaluation. Like the teacher, they too need opportunities to try things out and to struggle along the way.

Obviously, teaching the democratic way requires us to think about evaluation in ways quite different from those typically used in classrooms. The premium here is on encouraging students to think carefully about their own work, to have a meaningful say in assessing it, to reflect on how democratic values are integrated into group work, and to take the lead in reporting how their work went. Many educators would no doubt say that they would love to do these things if only there was time enough in their already busy classrooms. The fact is that every teacher spends a lot of time doing grades and report cards. The democratic way of evaluating is not so much about time as about a commitment to the idea that young people have a right and responsibility to reflect on their efforts. Instead of asking where we will find the time, we would do better to ask what the consequences are of young people learning to depend entirely on others for judgments about what and how they do. And there is nothing new about this. I recently came across a letter from my own school days fifty years ago explaining to parents the self-evaluation documents that we did to accompany our report cards. Its reasoning is still relevant today:

> These reports, a cooperative pupil-teacher effort, try to give parents some additional information about the work habits, attitudes and abilities of pupils. Each pupil, in conference with the teacher, attempts to evaluate progress toward a set of goals which each class sets for itself. The process of evaluation is exacting and time consuming. We feel that the effort is worthwhile to the pupil, to the parent, and to the school.

Achievement and Democracy

In the first chapter, I argued for a democracy in which social justice and equity are taken seriously. For this reason, educators who want to teach the democratic way are in a constant search for high achievement for all young people, especially those who are non-privileged and for whom difficulty in school cannot be offset by family wealth or influence. Importantly, all of the methods and approaches I have already described offer more access to more knowledge for more young people. Along with the democratic classroom policies I will suggest in the next chapter, those in this one are inviting, engaging, in-depth, and comprehensive.

Even so, critics often dismiss these methods as lacking "rigor." They may be right if they mean typical dictionary definitions of *rigor* that use terms like "harsh, "inflexible in opinion," "severe," and "tyrannical." After all, those terms certainly do not hint at democracy. But if we use "rigor" to refer to methods that are intellectually stimulating, involve high expectations, and require in-depth inquiry, the critics would be quite wrong. The methods I have described meet this definition much more than the rote drill, textbook exercises, constant lecturing, and simplistic worksheets forced on young people in too many classrooms. Could the critics possibly want young people to have experiences that match the typical dictionary definition of *rigor*? I hope not, for in those dictionaries, *rigor* is usually immediately preceded by the term *rigamorole*, defined as "a complex and largely meaningless procedure," and then followed immediately by *rigor mortis*.

Teaching the democratic way means pushing for those higher expectations and more rigorous learning experiences. It also means differentiating instruction, encouraging different learning styles, and otherwise accounting for the diversity among young people. In a democratic society, we should want all young people to experience the best education we have to offer while recognizing that all may not approach or engage with it in the same way. In this sense, accounting for diversity involves variety within a heterogeneous group rather than separate groupings or different curriculum content for different students.

This issue is becoming increasingly important as our most nonprivileged young people are drilled over and over with menial worksheets about bits and pieces of skill and information meant to prepare them for standardized tests. Often this fact of school life, especially in large urban areas, is a result of educators believing that poor children need that kind of "structure" for orderly classroom learning to occur. Sometimes, though, it is the parents of nonprivileged children themselves who insist on using those methods in the belief that they are the only way to get what is necessary to pass standardized tests. And who can blame these parents? When standardized tests carry such high stakes and have historically worked against nonprivileged children, any teaching method that appears to depart even slightly from the teaching of facts and skills would be cause for alarm. Ironically, though, research on teaching methods associated with democratic practices consistently shows that they are associated with success on standardized tests (Beane 1997; Marks, Newmann, and Gamoran 1996; Thomas 2000). Given this, how could it be that teachers using democratic methods do not engage children with the "stuff" that is on standardized tests? Or is it more that when they talk about their classrooms, they emphasize other, higher-level kinds of learning like thinking and problem solving?

> *The possibility of democratic reform lies with citizens who choose equality as the standard of social progress and the measure of their own empowerment.*
> Ann Bastian et al., 1986

Meanwhile, the premium ways of learning, like those I have described in this chapter, are left to the good fortune of more privileged young people whose economic and cultural standing alone prepares them for most standardized tests. Why do educators, policy makers, and legislators seem to favor the least effective teaching practices for the least privileged children, even manipulating research to support their views? Why wouldn't they want the best practices for everyone?

Not too long ago, I watched as a young man arrived at a new school after moving from one of the poorest cities in the nation. His teacher in the new school placed a premium on problem solving, hands-on activities, discussion, and other rigorous and engaging methods in a well-organized heterogeneous classroom. Sadly, her new student had no idea what to do in this new situation. Indeed, he had no way of even understanding it, since in all his previous years of school, he had never been in such a setting. His experience was all about drill and worksheets and simplistic activities and trivial content. Where is the equity in that? Where is the justice? What could policy makers and legislators be thinking when they encourage such inequity through their testing programs and unfair funding practices? Why would they allow such undemocratic practices to persist in schools meant to promote democracy? I will give these questions more attention in the last chapter. But we should never leave a discussion of democratic teaching without saying that the press for achievement is part of it. After all, in a democratic society, young people have a right to expect their schools to offer them the best chance for success.

The Teacher's Role

For some educators, picturing a classroom in which students are involved in planning, group work, discussion, self-evaluation, and other democratic practices suggests that the teacher has simply lost all direction and authority. Nothing could be further from the truth. Teaching the democratic way requires tremendous teacher presence and skill as well as a solid understanding about how to prepare for discussions of social issues (Hess 2002).

In a democratic classroom, students and teachers do not simply follow a textbook or prescribed lessons. Their work involves thinking, problem solving, researching, evaluating, and other complex activities. Sophisticated as many young people seem to be, they do not necessarily know how to pose powerful questions, critically examine information, conduct thorough research, debate an issue, or prepare complete projects. Nor do they necessarily know what the larger society expects them to learn or what issues and problems are prominent outside their own locales. For this reason, the teacher is especially important in a democratic classroom to be certain that crucial questions are raised, persistent problems recognized, an array of sources consulted, and information and skills applied. Moreover, the teacher must be able to integrate externally mandated curriculum standards, no matter how insignificant they may be, into the context of units and activities that involve significant social problems and issues.

At the same time, however, teaching the democratic way means constantly questioning what it means to be democratic in the classroom: When do I intervene? How hard do I press here? Should I say something or let the group figure it out? For questions like these, there in no curriculum package, no prescribed lesson, no script, no certain and final answer. Instead there are only the ever-present questions that challenge the attempt to create a democratic community and curriculum.

It is the teacher's job to help young people think more deeply, more broadly, and more critically. If the teacher were not crucial, we could simply hire people off the streets to teach our children. Where little is expected of students, that may sometimes seem feasible. But teaching the democratic way is not easy, and much is expected of students. Given the importance of democracy and the way it is misused and misunderstood these days, the stakes are high. To meet this challenge, we need very good teachers—and they certainly cannot afford to fade into the classroom background.

At the End of the Day

Educators spend a lot of time looking in the professional mirror, reflecting on what went well and what didn't, why students did or did not do well with some test, why they did or didn't seem to engage with some activity, and on and on. Those committed to teaching the democratic way are no exception. Having explored some of the things they do in the classroom, we can expect that besides the usual kinds of teaching questions, they ask others that have to do with bringing democracy to life:

- Did my students have an adequate and appropriate voice in classroom planning?
- Was the content we focused on of some social significance?
- Were students involved in rigorous and authentic activity?
- Did we consult a variety of sources and viewpoints in our research?
- Did we critically examine information and viewpoints?
- How could our work extend more often into community service?
- Did we use a variety of ways to reflect on and evaluate our work and our group?
- Did students have an adequate and appropriate say in creating our evaluation?
- Did students have an adequate voice in evaluating their own work?
- Were my expectations high enough, and did I push all students to do well?
- Was there enough variety in activities and materials so that all students had an equitable chance to access the curriculum?
- Did I play out my role as teacher in a democratic way?

More of us ought to ask ourselves these kinds of questions. If we did, perhaps we would also see a lot more examples of teaching the democratic way.

Throughout this chapter, I have described many different ways of teaching the democratic way as well as numerous examples. The chapter ends with a wonderful account of democratic education in which teacher Brian Schultz and his young students took on a real and significant problem in their lives and used it as the organizing center for their work over an extended period of time. It is an example that deserves our undivided attention, first because it brings together many of the very best ideas for democratic teaching and second because their project was carried out in one of the poorest and most neglected neighborhoods in the United States.

Spectacular Things Happen Along the Way

Brian D. Schultz

The noise level amplified in Room 405. The students were shouting out ideas as I quickly tried to keep up with their growing list. The intensity was beyond measurement as students called out problems that affected them: "teenage pregnancy," "litter in the park," even "stopping Michael Jackson!" A lot of the problems had to do with the school: "foggy windows pocked with bullet holes," "no lunchroom, gym or auditorium," "clogged toilets" and "broken heaters in the classroom." Before it was all said and done, these fifth graders had identified 89 different problems that affected them and their community, a challenge I had posed to them just an hour prior.

As the list grew and I hurriedly marked up the chalkboard with their ideas, some students began arguing with one another that a problem they proposed had already been mentioned. Insightfully, Shaniqua cut through the ensuing debate and stated, "Most of the problems on that list have to do with our school building bein' messed up. Our school is a dump! That's the problem." With this profound analysis there was a sense of affirmation in the room, and the students unanimously agreed the most pressing issue was the poor condition and inadequacy of their school building. The irony confronted me as I looked out at the group of students gathered together on that cold December morning. Most were wearing hats, gloves and coats in the classroom, personifying the real problem they were living. They were very perceptive in citing the numerous problems having to do with the school. These students knew them well; they had lived this injustice their entire school-aged lives.

In short order, these fifth graders listed major problems in need of fixing. In posing the question, I had anticipated the students might decide on simpler tasks like "wanting fruit punch at lunch" or trying to "get recess every day." Instead they went for a more challenging issue, one that had been in the community for years: a new school had been promised but was never built. I wondered to myself, were these students really willing to take this problem head-on? Before I could even ask, they were already coming up with ways they could possi-

Our school is not safe, comfortable or a good place to learn because of all these things wrong with it. (Taken from project website)

bly remedy some of the problems with the school structure and constructing plans to get a new school built. Given the opportunity and challenge to prioritize a problem in their community, the children were not only willing to itemize the issues, but were already strategizing ways to act and make changes. And so this emergent curriculum began.

Framing the Situation

As I teach and learn with my students who reside in Chicago public housing, I continually affirm my notion that the role of the teacher is to provide opportunity and space to students. The teacher ultimately must embrace intelligence and allow students to leverage what they know and what they already can successfully accomplish. As the students develop this essential opportunity, their imagination, interest, and creativity allow them to create a love for their learning that will endure the travesties and injustices they face both outside and inside the classroom.

In Chicago's Near North side is one of the most infamous housing projects in the country. Notorious for drugs and gangs, and synonymous with failing social programs and Great Society initiatives meant to help low-income citizens, Cabrini Green was first constructed in the early 1940s as temporary housing for a diverse group of poor residents. As time went on, and for a variety of social reasons, the temporary housing concept fell through and the red and white high-density tenement buildings and accompanying row houses became permanent homes for the children and their families. The badly maintained buildings were an eyesore and their mismanagement became symbolic of urban blight and everything wrong with public housing in this country. Now comprised of 99 percent African American families, the residences have become so dilapidated and deteriorated that the housing authority has declared them unlivable.

The Chicago Housing Authority's plan to redevelop the area and make it available for mixed-income families has created a hotbed of controversy as gentrification efforts and the displacement of poor black children and their families occurs. A critical problem with this plan is that instead of making the new development accessible to its current residents, the city and housing authority are uprooting the African American residents out of this high profile, largely sought after land, which sits in the shadows of the luxurious buildings of the affluent Gold Coast neighborhood.

Almost every account I have read about Chicago's poverty-stricken Cabrini Green describes the area as a haven for drugs and murder, gang-banging, misery and mayhem. Even in an article lauding my students' work, the author insisted that "Cabrini Green has all the stuff of which failure is made, and it often delivers door-to-door" (Brady 2004). Much of this portrayal may be accurate, but the story of these people, especially the children is rarely told. Within this community there are young kids with many needs. They require the same or better instruction, dedication, and nurturing as any other student in any other area. In addition, these students are capable citizens and thinkers with untapped creativity needing the opportunity to demonstrate and practice their intelligences. Darnell said this idea better than I could ever write it: "Even though our neighborhood has problems, we are proud of our neighborhood. This is why we are fighting for a better school. We think everyone should have a good home and a good school. Don't you agree?"

Because of the challenging conditions associated with the Cabrini Green ghetto, coupled with societal issues and constraints, the perennial question of *what is worth knowing* is raised constantly for my students. An understanding of how students from this neighborhood learn is imperative, as they continually adapt in a practical, pragmatic sense. Prior to our time together, they told me, there was little nurturing of the strengths or abilities learned out-of-school, but rather a devaluing of their adaptive and street intelligences. Many could not endure life in the projects without "bein' street smart or learnin' how to survive . . . because there are a lot of people who are gonna test you." At the same time they are seldom recognized in the school setting for their achievements outside of the classroom. If education was measured by the students' successes in their neighborhood via their own lived experiences, many would out-perform their more affluent peers. As I pondered this situation, I wondered how I might best be able to use their adaptability and street savvy in school. Could an emergent, authentic and integrated curriculum that focused on students' interests and concerns be successful in the "traditional" classroom?

Documenting and Reaching Out

We began by documenting the problems in the school by taking photographs and writing expository text about its shortfalls. The students produced compositions that were astonishing. I could not believe the level of sophistication in their writing. When asked how they were able to construct such amazing work on a rough draft, Tyrone responded, "This stuff is really important and I need to get the word out if I want something done." These rough drafts became the starting point, and getting the word out is exactly what they did. Quickly realizing that their drafts needed to be transformed into persuasive statements, the students compiled their individual work to create a powerful letter that was sent to school board and city officials, newspaper reporters and concerned citizens. In this letter the students documented "the big problems" about their school that were "not fixable" and promptly stated, "We would like to invite you to see our school for yourself. We do not think you would let your kids come to a school that is falling apart." And with this provocative invitation, the stage was set for an adventure none of us will soon forget.

Responses came pouring in immediately. Phone inquires, letters, emails, and visits from legislators as well as newspaper and TV reporters kept the students' project flowing with questions, suggestions, and encouragement. In reaching out beyond the four walls of the classroom, the students became quickly engaged in real-life curricula. As the class made their concerns known, many people offered insight, assistance, donations and the much-needed publicity. Taking into account advice from these outsiders, the students put together a comprehensive action plan that they believed would "help us get our perfect solution . . . a whole new school."

The students' action plan became the epicenter of the entire curriculum for the remainder of the school year. Every subject lost its compartmentalization and became integrated and integral in solving the problem of getting an "equal" school. Reading, writing, arithmetic and social studies were all blended in a natural way. Rather than using basal textbooks the students researched pertinent information about how to solve their problem. Their search took them to texts that went beyond their reading level and aptitude, but they were willing to put forth the effort because it had value to their situation. While reading from Jonathan Kozol's *Savage Inequalities,* Chester appropriately remarked, "I think this book was written 'bout us. The author must of come to Byrd school." And Chester's statement was not far from the truth, as Shaquita and Marquis documented, "The restrooms are filthy and dirty. It is really smelly in the bathrooms because the toilets don't flush. As an example of how bad they are, sinks move and water leaks on the floor. The sinks have bugs in them and water leaks everywhere. And we do not even have soap or paper towels.

Figure 2–4

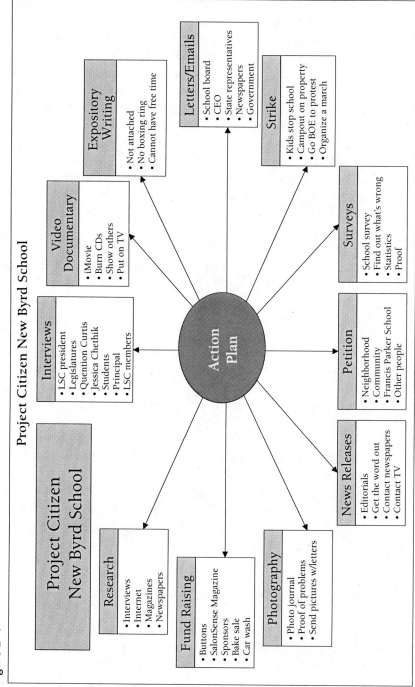

Project Citizen New Byrd School

Project Citizen New Byrd School

Action Plan

Research
• Interviews
• Internet
• Magazines
• Newspapers

Fund Raising
• Buttons
• SalonSense Magazine
• Sponsors
• Bake sale
• Car wash

Photography
• Photo journal
• Proof of problems
• Send pictures w/letters

News Releases
• Editorials
• Get the word out
• Contact newspapers
• Contact TV

Petition
• Neighborhood
• Community
• Francis Parker School
• Other people

Surveys
• School survey
• Find out what's wrong
• Statistics
• Proof

Strike
• Kids stop school
• Campout on property
• Go BOE to protest
• Organize a march

Letters/Emails
• School board
• CEO
• State representatives
• Newspapers
• Government

Expository Writing
• Not attached
• No boxing ring
• Cannot have free time

Video Documentary
• iMovie
• Burn CDs
• Show others
• Put on TV

Interviews
• LSC president
• Legislatures
• Quention Curtis
• Jessica Chethik
• Students
• Principal
• LSC members

Kids don't use it in the bathrooms no more since they are so gross and falling apart."

Reading flowed into current events as students read and reacted to newspaper articles written about their work. In addition they read about techniques for participation, which "showed us how to do things like survey and petition." The students learned how to prepare documentation including their survey results, photos, and written assessments as they incorporated data analysis and mathematics into their student-driven curriculum to gain support. After taking this documentation to the public, Danisha asserted, "No one who saw our folders could disagree with what we were saying about the school's problems." Their willingness and fervor in understanding and making sense of the text went beyond my wildest expectations. The students felt they needed to "get more folks involved and aware" so they developed a website (www.projectcitizen405.com) to "organize all the stuff." This was no small task as they had pictures and writing from visits of politicians and researchers, hundreds of letters and emails written on their behalf, journal entries, petitions, charts, graphs, surveys and analyses.

Room 405 became the headquarters to "make important decisions about who we should bring in to help" and was a think-tank for investigating ways "we can better get others involved." The classroom transformed into a campaign office. The students assumed roles of leadership in their quest and as Kamala commented in his journal, "Being an interviewer . . . makes me feel like a business manager. . . . It makes me feel real important and other kids look up to me. This has never happened to me in school before." The eager students were so involved in the development of their curriculum they often came early and left late and even came in on their days off to "get the job done."

"Reactions Came Rollin'"

Their initiative and perseverance paid off. Although there was some disappointment and frustration in not getting an immediate response from "the decision makers at the board of education and the city," other people certainly responded, hearing the cries for equity in schooling. From local legislators visiting and lobbying on the students' behalf, to inquiries and case studies of university professors interested in writing about the project, to concerned citizens like Ralph Nader paying visits, the students were applauded and awarded for their fine work. At times, though, I was accused of "being behind this" because, as a Chicago Public School official stated, "There was no way that kids from Byrd school were capable of doing work like this . . . we have gotten too many letters." I may have been guilty of being behind my students, but they were the ones fighting to solve their problem, not me. Such comments were frequently made since many people simply could not believe that these "inner city, black kids" were capable of doing such amazing work. As Crown commented, "We are finally getting on the news for somethin' good!" And this recognition was truly the most important. The students began believing in themselves and understanding their capabilities. As they worked through the issues of their project, they realized they may not get what they were asking for, but the "process was the best part because people listened to us and agreed with us."

The students' efforts did get results. In a classroom that had vastly diverse abilities and aptitudes, students worked at their own pace and took on various roles so as to have the most impact on the outcome of their plans. They were not affected by peers' progress or limitations, but rather sought out opportunities that allowed them to feel comfortable working together while at the same time also stepping out of their individual comfort zones when ready. Prior to engaging in the project, few students valued their learning as typified by many failing to participate in classroom activities, not completing homework, and being frequently absent from school.

Over the many months of the project, the standardized test scores of most students increased over the previous year, several significantly, without direct time spent on test prep. Discipline problems simply did not exist, and attendance was at a sky-high 98 percent. In addition to their high achievement and although they never directly received any response from the decision makers, some of their listed problems within the school were remedied. Items that the school engineer had been asking to have fixed for years were all of a sudden getting the attention they had lacked. Lights were replaced, doors were fixed, and soap dispensers were even put into the bathrooms!

But, "not satisfied with stupid band-aids," as Reggie put it, the students continued their fight and also continued being recognized. Letters of support kept on coming, a case was established with the U.S. Department of Education, the Illinois State Board of Education invited the students to Springfield, and the Center for Civic Education had the students present at their national convention for Project Citizen. They received numerous awards and "project of the year" designations from the Constitutional Rights Foundation and Northwestern University. Called "young warriors" and compared to "civil rights freedom fighters of the 1960s," they were empowered and uplifted by the response of "people willing to help us that don't even know us."

Now awakened, the young people's intelligence and inspiration, interest and imagination certainly drove their learning. Instead of relying on me to create lesson plans that tailored and contrived different activities, the students had the responsibility to figure out what was most important to solving this problem. They were discovering the most worthwhile knowledge and it was coming from within them. Instead of focusing on memorization and rote learning, the students were naturally meeting standards of excellence because it was necessary for solving the authentic problem at hand. Their action plan forced them to interact with each other and with a system that could potentially help them solve the problem identified. As each student self-selected various roles in order to enact the parts of the plan, their efforts came to life and the public's reaction became more intense. In order to make progress and get the attention they needed, the students' rigor naturally met the standards and objectives expected by the city and state. In fact, their efforts went well beyond any standards or prescriptions because they wanted and needed to learn the skills necessary in order to actively participate in their project.

Looking Back

Frustrated by a hidden curriculum based on social class, I was looking for a compromise that would keep my students motivated and engaged in their learning, while at the same time teaching them the necessary skill-base to progress in school. Challenging the accepted notion of teaching socioeconomic classes differently, I sought the equity in teaching and learning that I so strongly felt my students deserved. My initial wondering led me to revisit the perennial questions with my students: "What knowledge is most worthwhile? Why is it worthwhile? How is it acquired or created?" (Schubert 1986, 1). What would happen if, in Room 405 at Byrd Community Academy, in one of the most perilous housing projects in the country, we took on an experiment of our own? What if the students were given the space to problem-pose, challenge, and deliberate like their counterparts in more affluent schools rather than simply being expected to follow the rules and give the right answers as they usually were? Would the experiment prove to be a disaster, would the children be squashed by the system, or would this curriculum prove successful? Could the teacher and students share authority in the classroom working together in practical and cooperative inquiry? Could the curriculum be driven by student interest to meet situational needs? Would we be able to go beyond following the rules and assert creative ideals? Could we challenge the status quo to make the curriculum of, for and by us? Or as one of the girls in the class asked, "Who's gonna listen to a bunch of black kids from Cabrini Green?" There was only one way to find out.

Using these questions as a framework for a democratic curriculum, and inspired by a Project Citizen workshop (Center for Civic Education), the students embarked on an experience in learning how the government works and ways they might "be active agents in bringing about social change" (Cobb 1991). As I now look back, I remember a conversation with several students in which one, Sharnell, summarized our work in the classroom as a "way to learn how the government works and ways to work the government." By embracing a meaningful problem, the curriculum became a catalyst for authentic, natural, and integrated learning to occur.

Through the project, the students were given the opportunity and responsibility to be active participants in the development and design of their own learning. The comments of Tavon, who was a chronic truant prior to participating in this

Teacher Brian Schultz and part of the Project Citizen 405 group.

classroom resonate strongly: "I did not feel school was a place for me. I didn't think it would help me in my life, but this project made me like coming to school. . . . It did not feel like the boring school I was used to." His turnaround and new-found dedication to schoolwork and attendance demonstrates the power of a democratic classroom where all students are critical members and are allowed to embrace their own ideas of what is worthwhile.

As their teacher, I learned that content can come from the students rather than be driven into them by forcibly preparing concrete objectives in an artificial manner. Just as students in the more affluent schools are encouraged and rewarded for their insight and creativity, these urban, African American students now could have their voices heard through purposeful action and determination. And in this particular case, their voices were no longer silenced.

There are certainly risks involved in trying to solve authentic curriculum problems and create democratic ideals in a classroom. Students are no longer protected by contrived lesson plans and people will cast doubt as to whether students, especially inner city African Americans, are capable of taking on a real problem. Even the school's extremely supportive principal initially had reservations about the lessons they might learn from the project. In a National Public Radio interview he said, "If they don't see things happening, I am afraid that they are going to say, voice all you want, but your voice is a small voice and doesn't matter." Today, though, everyone, including the principal, would argue the lessons that were taken away from the project are immeasurable. Tamika succinctly summed up this idea in a journal entry, "We would love to get our perfect solution of getting a new school built, but we have figured out that great things can happen when you fight for what is right. . . . Even though we are not getting a new school we have done great things . . . like it said in one of the letters supporting us, 'Spectacular things happen along the way!'"

As I write this a year later, I am still in contact with many of my former students. The curriculum the students and I developed together has had a lasting impact on all of us. Opportunities to tell our story continue to emerge. While putting this account together, I thought it was essential and appropriate to involve students in some dialogue about how the piece sounded and to give me feedback about the writing. As I went through the text with one boy, Tywon, I asked him, "Who am I as a white, middle-class teacher to write about you guys?" Tywon looked me directly in the eye and said, "To me you ain't speaking outta turn because you not talkin' bad or nothin' about black people . . . you taking they side and feelin' what they feelin."

This account was prepared with the help of several former Byrd Community Academy students, including Tywon Easter, Manuel Pratt, and Lamarius Brewer.

3 Living the Democratic Way

On the day before my oldest son started fifth grade, we walked to the school to see what his new classroom would be like. Knowing the fifth-grade teacher, I imagined a colorfully decorated, welcoming room with desks organized in small groups. Instead I was surprised to find the room looking completely unlived in. The walls were bare, the desks in no particular order, and the shelves empty. When I asked the teacher to explain he said, "This room belongs to the group, not to me. We'll decide how it should look when we're all here tomorrow." What could I have been thinking?

At its core, democracy is a way we choose of being together with others, a way of living, learning, and making our lives better. Like any other community, a democratic community lives by certain norms regarding how people relate to each other and how things get done. Over time, these norms create a democratic culture in the community. What does a democratic culture look like in a classroom? How do people get along? What do they expect of each other? How are decisions made? What is the role of the teacher? What are some ways of moving toward a more democratic culture in the classroom?

Given the emphasis that democracy places on freedom and participation, schools may seem like odd places to talk about in terms of the democratic way. After all, school attendance is compulsory rather than voluntary, school authorities are appointed rather than

> *A democracy is more than a form of government; it is primarily a mode of associated living.*
> John Dewey, 1916

elected by the young people who are the school's main constituency, and broad goals for students (and teachers) are largely predetermined by people outside the school. Moreover, a strong argument can be made for such arrangements in a democratic society. For one thing, creating some kind of social fabric requires some level of common education. For another, even though the schools have not been all that successful at leveling the social and economic playing field, without them, social mobility for non-privileged youth would be almost completely left to chance. And tempting as it may sometimes seem to turn the schoolhouse upside down and empty everyone out, it is hard to imagine how schools could begin to get any better without having a stable and well-prepared profession to sustain them. Finally, the fact that school goals set by federal, state, and local authorities are often wrong-headed does not diminish the idea that the larger society maintains schools to accomplish important societal goals. Helping young people to learn the democratic way of living supposedly is the most important, even though it seems to have fallen so far out of fashion these days.

But even setting those laws and social imperatives aside, schools are still filled with policies and procedures that seem to contradict the possibilities of democracy. While school goals speak of students learning democratic citizenship, becoming independent, and thinking critically, the reality inside the schools suggests something quite different. Increasingly, the school curriculum is set even before teachers and students meet each other, and the knowledge it demands belongs to subject specialists and textbook authors far removed from the classroom. Classroom decisions are still made almost entirely by teachers, with little or no student voice. Rules, schedules, and groupings are set before the students arrive. And for young people, evaluation of their work and life inside the school is done by almost everyone except themselves, from teachers to test makers.

As with the term *democracy* itself (see Chapter 1), I struggle with what to call those kinds of policies and procedures. Calling them "undemocratic" seems a bit harsh, especially when there is no one set recipe for doing things the democratic way. Moreover, schools that use such policies and procedures may contain some elements of the democratic way like heterogeneous grouping. Calling them "traditional," as is often done, would be a mistake, since democratic schools and teaching have a long and rich tradition of their own. Perhaps it is most appropriate to refer to such policies and procedures simply as "the usual way of doing things" or, for short, "the usual way." After all, those policies and procedures are the dominant way things have been done for so long and in so many places that most people seem to see them as the only way to do things.

So deeply rooted is this "usual way" in the life and lore of our society that even television and movie producers are confident that we will immediately recognize certain characters and situations: the authoritarian teacher, the alienated student, the irrelevant curriculum, and the lifeless classroom. Talk about any other way of doing things seems almost out of place and unrealistic. Challenges to the usual way are often put down with the admonition that "it has to be that way so we can get our kids ready for the real world"—or "the job market"—or "college." These kinds of remarks are a sad commentary on the current state of society and its educational institutions, since they suggest that schools can only be justified by their ties to self-interest, personal ambition, and corporate needs.

But what about getting young people ready to live in a democratic society or to help bring such a society back on course after it has lost its bearings? Does the usual way of doing things do that? The answer is no. To say otherwise would be like saying that young people will become readers by not reading or musicians by never picking up an instrument. We learn the democratic way of life by living it—by seeing and feeling how it works and how it can be nurtured as well as how it can be diminished. The preparation for living the democratic way is democracy.

And what about the rights of young people as citizens in a democratic society? Are those left behind when they arrive at school? Or is it an obligation of schools in a democratic society to recognize the citizen rights of young people? These are not simple questions. Policy makers, educators, and even the courts have long debated whether democratic rights extend to young people in schools. In cases involving censorship of school newspapers and access to public school facilities by private religious groups, the courts have most often recognized the school as a "limited public forum" in which the rights of students may be preempted by the fact that schools are social institutions and thus have to be concerned with personal privacy, equity, and other obligations. These long-running debates are an excellent example of how particular ideas are shaped and reshaped, over and over, in a democratic society.

So, how does a school decide what it should do with regard to democratic rights of young people? Too often, it seems that the answer is to avoid them altogether so as to keep things running smoothly and without controversy. But because a democratic society depends on its schools to promote democracy, a more sensible response would be to take the democratic rights of young people as far as possible in the one place where almost all of them come together. Wouldn't it make sense that when in doubt, schools in a democratic society would err on the side of democracy? What if we took seriously the right of young people to have a say, to have their opinions count, to be treated with dignity, and to be engaged in meaningful and significant activities? And what if we also took seriously the need to create opportunities where they might also exercise their democratic social obligations to pull their weight in the community, to lend a hand to others, and to speak up for their views? What might life inside the school and classroom look like?

Creating a Collaborative Community

Probably nothing is more frequently associated with the idea of democratic classrooms than the notion of creating a sense of community among it members, both students and teachers. This is hardly surprising, since democracy itself is partly based on the concept of individuals coming together in groups to address issues, solve problems, and pursue common purposes. The democratic classroom is not simply practice for that concept. It is an example of it.

The work of a democratic classroom begins with people coming to know each other in some authentic ways. Sharing information about themselves, interviewing each other, conducting in-class surveys about favorite activities, making personal timelines, going camping together, and similar activities are often used by teachers to help build relationships within classrooms. However, in the democratic classroom, forming relationships in these ways is not only a matter of getting along or improving climate. It is a step along the way to the kind of community that is necessary to take on important issues with a sense of collective strength and commitment.

One of the fundamental concepts of democracy is that communities of people determine how they will live together. This means thinking about rules, policies, and norms for actions and activities. Certain policies are given, of course, such as compulsory attendance and the prohibition of weapons and drugs. Some local districts also have policies insisting that schools be anti-racist, antisexist and, less commonly, antihomophobic as well. But this still leaves a number of decisions about day-to-day behaviors and activities open for consideration.

> *Democratic communities . . . should start in the classrooms in which students share responsibility for their own learning and for regulating each others' behavior.*
> Andy Hargreaves and Michael Fullan, 1998

At the classroom level, these decisions open the door for participation and collaboration. Democratic teachers find many ways to take advantage of the opportunity. Some organize daily or weekly class meetings with their students to consider how things are going and whether there are problems that ought to be taken up by the group. Others organize their classrooms around committees and student leaders who have responsibility for considering problems or issues that arise in the classroom. Still others begin the year by working with their students to construct a classroom "constitution" as a framework for group norms and decisions (see Figure 3–1). Often, especially with young children, the whole group discusses and reaches consensus on norms for group living. Another method involves having small groups of students brainstorm possible norms, bring those lists together, and then look for common ideas across the groups. Mark Springer, a middle-school teacher in Radnor, Penn-

Figure 3–1

Room 201/202 Constitution

We the class of Rooms 201/202, in order to form the best class possible, pledge to live by the following statements:

- We appreciate our individual differences. We recognize that each person is unique.
- All individuals will be treated with respect and dignity. There is no room for put-downs in our room.
- We will be honest with one another in order to build trust.
- We will learn to resolve conflicts, which may involve learning to live with nonresolution.
- Each person will truly listen to every other person.
- We will cooperate and collaborate with one another.
- Learning will be meaningful.
- We recognize that people learn in different ways.
- Assignments, field trips, hands-on experiences will be varied so that everyone can and will learn. If everyone tries, we *all* will succeed.
- Having fun will naturally become part of our experiences.
- All individuals will be organized and on time.
- We will respect the right to pass (not take a turn).

We agree to abide by these truths to the best of our abilities, both as unique individuals and as a cooperative and collaborative community.

(Brodhagen 1995)

---

sylvania, goes one step further, encouraging his students to use the federal Constitution as a template for organizing the group's ideas about how they will live together in the classroom. For those who have not tried this kind of thing before, teachers Katie Salkowski, Christine Mitlyng, and Lisa Underkofler offer this description of their first attempt:

> We created a classroom constitution so students would realize they had a voice in the classroom and take ownership of the classroom community. Our hope was to break down the idea

that teachers have all the power and to encourage students to think for themselves about their needs and desires for the year ahead. Creating a constitution would also open the door to talking about what people in communities need in order to live and to get along and how our team is a community. The students individually brainstormed what they needed to be a successful member of the learning community. Next they shared their individual ideas in small groups and listed items they had in common. With teacher guidance the small group lists were brought together in a whole team list. During this time there was a lot of discussion about whether or not a particular item was needed and why or why not. One item that came up was whether or not we needed to have a specific statement that our school district code of conduct would be followed. The students said that was a given and that they did not need it restated on our list.

Once the student list was complete we put up a list of "non-negotiable" things that we teachers felt we needed in order to teach. It was interesting to see how these "non-negotiables" meshed with what the students already had on their list and how we all wanted the same things for our classrooms. After a discussion about final wording we typed up the list so each person could have a copy and also made two **large copies to** post in each of our team's two classrooms. Finally **we sched-**uled a formal "Constitution signing" at which everyone who might be part of our community, including students, teachers, principal, assistant principal, and support staff all signed the two posted copies.

We refer to the Constitution when students are not meeting one or more of the statements by reminding them what the statements are. Students also remind each other (and sometimes the adults) when a constitution statement is not being followed. We call them "constitution statements" rather than "rules" in an effort to suggest a democratic, cooperative agreement rather than a punitive system and to remember that these are items everyone agreed they needed to live by rather than what the "person in power" needed.

Teachers who encourage this kind of collaborative decision making almost always report that their students are more committed to a "classroom constitution" than to a list of rules and procedures determined entirely by the teacher. Perhaps more importantly, they also report that students frequently use the

A democratic classroom community begins by deciding how to live together.

"constitution" throughout the year to resolve disputes and guide discussions about classroom climate. One teacher told me that after several units in which a group was involved with serious social issues and problems, some students pointed to the classroom constitution and reminded the teachers of the agreement that "we will work hard but we will also take time to have fun."

In Chapter 2, I warned against the undemocratic method by which some teachers involve students in curriculum planning as a way to "engineer" their consent toward a predetermined plan. The same holds true here. If we want to create anything close to a genuine democratic community in classrooms, we must approach collaborative planning with an open mind and without a predetermined agenda. This is not always easy to do, especially if we are trying to move away from the usual way of doing things. Eventually, we will become accustomed to the democratic way. But in the meantime, one rule of thumb might be this: *When the opportunity for collaborative community decision making knocks, the teacher's best bet is to open the door for students rather than trying to figure out what they might find inside.* That the students and teacher will discover together.

Creating classroom norms for behavior and activities is obviously not the only possibility for collaborative decision making. As my son's teacher so wisely pointed out, things like the arrangement of the room, the posting of material on the walls, and the arrangement of desks or tables might also be opened up for group deliberation. So, too, might matters like how small groups will be formed for some task, how portfolios will be stored, when to invite families for project exhibits—all of these and more are possibilities for the classroom community to decide how it will operate. In fact, there are so many opportunities when students might be involved in classroom decisions that a second rule of thumb is this: *If there is something you want to know, ask your students.*

There is one more rule of thumb that teachers have found helpful in moving toward more collaboration in decision making: *Teachers should try not to do things that students can do.* This rule might extend from organizing the classroom to planning the curriculum to running parent conferences. In a democratic community, people share the work and distribute power across the group. Participating in various roles and sharing responsibility is crucial if young people are to experience the opportunities and obligations of democracy. Remembering to turn things over to the students moves the community in that direction.

This rule is helpful in another way. For a number of reasons some students balk at the opportunity to be involved in planning. They may never have had the chance before, they may feel uncomfortable with the ambiguity, they may not fully trust the teacher, or they may simply not have any ideas to contribute. Sometimes these students demand that the teacher make the decisions, even saying, "That's what you get paid for!" How can we respond to that? One teacher I know uses a version of the "let the students do it" rule. She simply says, "I've already been to school. This is your turn to learn how to make decisions."

I do not want to leave the impression that the teacher is just another face in the crowd when it comes to determining norms for living in a democratic classroom. A democratic society maintains schools to promote the democratic way of life. Responsibility for that falls mainly into the hands of teachers, who bring to the classroom a wider range of experience and knowledge than do young people. Moreover, they are, in a very real sense, "employees" of the democratic society. Thus, teachers have an obligation to watch over the living arrangements made by the classroom community to ensure that they are fair and just and to intervene if they are not.

This is a very important idea for teachers who want to move toward teaching the democratic way. Doubting colleagues and other critics often belittle democratic teachers as irresponsible or careless for supposedly "letting the students do whatever they want." Though it may do little good, responding requires a reasoned argument about the role of the teacher in a democratic classroom. Ironically, of course, the critics of the democratic way rarely realize that by discounting the democratic way in someone else's classroom they are also saying something about their own. And that something suggests that perhaps they have not understood their obligations as teachers in a democratic society.

Respecting Dignity

Respect for human dignity is perhaps the most fundamental aspect of democracy, and for this reason it permeates the culture of democratic communities. When we teach the democratic way, we make the students' self-worth a central concern of classroom life. Democratic teachers not only come to know their students well. They also think about them in terms of what it means to be a young person in this place at this time.

In schools where the usual way of doing things prevails, students are just "students" and only that. The scope of their lives is defined by their role and place in school and how well they do in that role. Their goals, hopes, and aspirations are defined by what the school values: to succeed academically, to compete successfully against others, to find their place in the scheme of things. Lost in this portrait, however, are some very important facts. To begin with, young people are real people living real lives in the real world. The role of "student" is only one of many they play. They are also members of families, peer groups, and communities; citizens of the society; and participants in cultures that help shape their identities and values. They are of a particular age-group— children, young adolescents, and older adolescents—and are influenced by both the physical developments and the social and cultural expectations of their age. To respect the dignity of young

> *Each of our children, those with special education labels and those without them, call for us to understand— not ignore, to have compassion—not pity, to create community— not isolate.*
>
> Jean Ann Hunt, 2001

people means taking them seriously as whole human beings, not just as students. Who are these young people? What are their hopes and aspirations? What do they bring to school in terms of social and cultural experiences and identities? How old are they, and what expectations do school and society have for people that age? What is around them in terms of media messages, living conditions, community resources, and so on? Questions like these help us to see whole persons rather than just *students* in our classrooms. And when we do that, the door to respecting their dignity is opened.

And just beyond that view is the possibility of expanding our relationships with students, of seeing ourselves as coauthors of their education. They are no longer passive "students." They are people engaged in educative experiences. The lens through which we see them is their humanness rather than our subject area. We are able to see the experience, knowledge, and other strengths they bring to school rather than simply their skill deficits. We can begin to hear their voices, their hopes, their fears. And when this happens, we are more concerned about how they view themselves, how confident they feel, and how we might support them as young people. In this moment is the possibility of joining with students in a genuine democratic community, where teachers share with students all the decisions about how their community will be shaped, from the curriculum to social aspects to evaluation of all they do together.

As always, critics of the democratic way love to insist that such thinking leads teachers and students away from academic excellence and high expectations, as if knowing students well and teaching them well are mutually exclusive. The critics do not seem to understand that respecting the dignity of young people is crucial to having high expectations for them, for if I do not respect people, I am hardly likely to expect much from them. And more than that, the critics seem to forget that students are still human beings when they are in school and in that sense entitled to be treated with dignity. To do otherwise is decidedly undemocratic.

Prizing Diversity

Democracy has two great social dimensions. One is the "common good." The other is the individual needs, interests, and concerns that people bring to the community. Discussions of democracy usually emphasize the common good, perhaps because there seems to be more than enough self-centered thinking to go around. But the role of individuality in a democracy cannot be overestimated, for it is out of individual concerns and interests that those of the community are formed. And the more diverse the individuals, the richer and more promising the community, since diverse voices bring a wider range of opinions, ideas, and viewpoints. For this reason, diversity in a democratic classroom is seen as a strength rather than a problem. In teaching the democratic way, the purpose is not to make all students the same, but to enrich the community by building on the diversity of the group and by learning from, working with, and helping one another.

Teaching the democratic way involves helping young people come to know and appreciate the diversity within their classroom community. This means placing a premium on discussing different viewpoints on issues—considering different paths to follow to solve a problem, debating solutions to problems, and setting aside time for classroom meetings. It also means doing things like asking students to reflect on how they are the same as or different from others in the classroom, what strengths they bring to the group, and what they have learned from others. And sooner or later, it means consulting with students about what questions or concerns they bring to the classroom in general and to particular themes, topics, and projects.

> The lack of a genuine community of diversity is particularly evident in school curriculums that still do not regularly and systematically include important information and deep study about a wide range of diverse ethnic groups.
> Geneva Gay, 2003/2004

Teaching the democratic way also involves recognizing and drawing on diverse cultures. Certainly, the continuous search for literature, history, music, art, and other material from diverse cultures is crucial in creating a democratic culture in the classroom. Let's face it: A classroom in which artifacts of only one culture are used would hardly be conducive to living the democratic way;

omitting other cultures is undemocratic from the start. But beyond the use of multicultural materials are other possibilities. Teaching the democratic way also means introducing popular culture into the classroom, making space for students to bring issues and meanings from contemporary media and entertainment to the classroom. Too often, popular culture is shut out of classrooms in favor of classical, high-culture literature, music, art, and so on. Yet to say that popular culture is inappropriate for the classroom is to deny the potential importance of new ideas and forms of expression in understanding the world. It also tells young people in no uncertain terms that their cultural interests are irrelevant and insignificant.

Prizing diversity means making space for various learning styles, modes of expression, and so on. In a democratic community, we would certainly expect to hear a good deal of verbal activity in the form of discussion and debate. But if we prize diversity, we would also expect to see evidence of respect for different ways of knowing as students access knowledge through visual media, drama, or physical activities such as dance or games. The same variety of possibilities would also be available for students to display or "perform" what they have learned in different ways through portfolios, exhibitions, and demonstrations.

All of this may seem very far from the sometimes tense politics of multiculturalism in a democratic society. But it really isn't. These very practical ideas bring to life in the classroom the general principle of prizing diversity in a democratic culture. So, too, do structural arrangements such as heterogeneous grouping that tell students every day that the school recognizes and appreciates the differences in background, culture, viewpoints, knowledge, and skills that they bring to school. And rather than seeing these as a problem to be overcome by separating students or demanding they all be the same, such arrangements signal clearly that diversity is a strength on the road to a truly democratic community in which diverse young people live and work together.

The Classroom as Court of Knowledge

Sustaining democracy requires that people inquire into events, issues, and ideas so that they are well informed when making decisions or resolving problems. It also requires that they inquire with an open mind, a critical eye, and access to a wide range of information. For this reason, a democratic culture is a culture of inquiry in which good questions are more important than easy answers, and where figuring things out is more important than simply accumulating information.

One sign that a classroom is becoming a democratic community is when the group begins to organize around significant questions and issues. Typically, these come from two sources. One is the lived experience of members of the classroom community. As we saw in the previous chapter, there are a number of ways of involving students in curriculum planning with the purpose of using their questions and concerns to define themes and topics. The second source is the teacher's experience in the world. Even in the most sophisticated situations where students are involved in curriculum planning, teachers still actively make suggestions to the group. After all, given the limits of age and experience, students are not always aware of significant issues in the world. For example, in one all-white community in which we asked young people to identify questions and concerns they had about the world, almost everyone mentioned environmental issues, while none named racism or issues related to cultural diversity. In this case, the teachers had not only a right but also an obligation to bring these latter issues to the curriculum either through an explicit theme or by integrating them into other themes. Either way, though, teaching the democratic way involves posing questions and exploring ways of answering them.

> Every effort must be made in childhood to teach the young to use their own minds. For one thing is sure: If they don't make up their own minds, someone will do it for them.
> Eleanor Roosevelt

Obviously, this is quite different from the culture of classrooms where things are done the usual way. There the curriculum is organized around accumulating information. In a sense, that information also involves answering questions. However, these are not questions about significant self and social issues. Rather they are about what a few select individuals—a curriculum committee, professors, state education officials—believe young people ought to know before they graduate from school. This is not to say that such knowledge is always insignificant. The point is that in a democracy, people have a right to define the issues that should be addressed. The alienation of young people in too many classrooms is most often blamed on their own apathy. Sometimes it is attributed to the lack of engaging activities. Could it be that a large measure of the alienation has to do with the fact that students rarely have a voice in deciding which questions drive the curriculum? And feeling powerless in that way, could it be that they are unmoved by answers to questions they did not ask or are not even aware of? In the search for a democratic classroom culture, these are very important issues.

If a democratic community is to carry out its work intelligently, its members must have access to a wide range of information so that they can respond to significant questions and issues. Few things are so prized in a democracy as the right to be informed by access to a free flow of information and different viewpoints. Amy Gutmann (1987, 42) calls this the principle of "nonrepression"—providing people free access to information so that they may "deliberate rationally among differing ways of life." Teaching the democratic way means respecting that right and working for that access. This is why teachers who want democratic communities in their classrooms encourage their students to look beyond their textbooks to additional resources inside and outside the school.

Moreover, they push to bring diverse viewpoints into the classroom even when those viewpoints are unpopular or controversial. My colleague Mark Strebel has continuously pointed out that as technology has made all kinds of information readily available, it is more and more futile to act as if young people are not aware of what is going on in even the most unsavory corners of society. Beyond that, though, acting as if young people are ignorant of the world, especially popular culture and controversial topics, is to deny that they live in the world. It is also a dangerous start toward denying them access to knowledge that democratic citizenship requires.

The culture of inquiry in a democratic classroom, framed by questions and fed by wide-ranging information, eventually leads to questions of equity and justice. When people raise questions about significant issues, they almost always end up asking why things are the way they are. In a democracy, there is no other way. This level of inquiry opens yet another door for the curriculum. An excellent example involves a unit that is popular in all grades from elementary through high school in which students study advertising in commercial media. Typically, these units involve really good activities, such as keeping logs of television viewing, conducting surveys of favorite commercials, learning how commercials are made, and eventually making a simulated commercial for some new product. Sometimes students also debate the claims made by advertisers and discuss commercials as a form of propaganda. But there is another level of questioning that is less often explored. Why are commercial advertisers so interested in the "youth market"? Why are certain commercial advertisements designed with young people in mind? What assumptions do advertisers make about young people? Why are selected products cycled off the market and replaced by new ones? Who makes those decisions, and how?

Units that are full of questions like these remind us that what we call "knowledge" does not arise full-blown from some mystical vacuum. It is produced and created by real people based on what they observe, believe, and value. That human perception of events and issues may vary is taken for granted every day in courts of law where different people tell different versions of the same event. In legal court, we always figure that there are at least two sides to every story. Why not in the "court of knowledge"? Why in our classrooms do we assume that what our texts, media, and other resources tell us is anything more than someone's perspective on things? Maybe the information presented *is* true. But more likely there is also some other version of "the facts," as Howard Zinn (1980), James Loewen (1995), and the Rethinking Schools group (Bigelow and Peterson 1991) have amply demonstrated in their critical looks at events in U.S history.

Freedom to learn is surely one of the basic freedoms in a democracy.
Earl Kelley, 1962

Critical analysis of the media is not the only way to examine how "the facts" get manipulated. Examples can even be found within areas like mathematics, which most people seem to believe "objective" and thus beyond manipulation. But what does it mean to be told that the average person is a particular height and weight, wears a particular size clothing, and is expected to live a particular span of years? Such statements, heard every day, are quite different from saying that a particular group of people have an average height, weight, clothing size, and life expectancy. The difference? One does little beyond telling us some statistical information about a particular group. The other produces an image of an "average person," a symbol of what is "normal" and "expected." One informs us, the other attempts to shape our perceptions. Are people really that vulnerable? Take a look around. Democratic teachers and their students look into such manipulations.

In *The Long Revolution,* Raymond Williams (1961) reminds us of what he calls the "selective tradition," by which certain facts, events, people, literature, music, and so on, survive the political and cultural process and emerge as what is taken as important about a particular time. Teachers who choose to teach the democratic way wonder about that process all the time and remind their students to wonder as well. In a democracy, what is taken for fact is open to constant questioning so as to get the story of our lives and our world straight. Those who criticize such questioning as too complicated or too picky need only be reminded that at one time it was taken as fact that the world was flat. Wineburg and Martin (2004) remind us that the need for critical inquiry is especially important because distortions of history on the Internet and in the popular media threaten to misinform young people, who take everyone at their word.

Examples like these push the curriculum into "critical ethics," an arena as important to democratic living as it may be controversial in school politics. In a democracy, we do not simply assume that things are as they appear to be on the surface. We want to know what lies behind the scenes and why things are the way they are. Although adults are often annoyed by children who never stop asking why, we should celebrate that these children are already showing the search for understanding that is a hallmark of democratic living. And when we take the time to answer those questions—including the questions coming from young children—we are teaching the democratic way.

On the other hand, hardly anything can make more trouble for teachers and students than digging into social events and issues around them. Some critics say that school students are too young for this kind of thing and should be shielded from what may be unpleasant information. Others claim that it takes valuable time away from "more important" activities. Too often, though, what these critics really mean is that they simply don't want these kinds of questions asked in the classroom because students may, in fact, become critical rather than passive participants in society. This seems an odd criticism in a democratic society. Certainly, there is no shortage of demand for "character education" in the schools; and in a democratic society, hardly anything would seem more in character than questions that explore ethics in the world around us.

Unfortunately, the call for character education in recent years has given rise mostly to a variety of slogan-centered programs supposedly intended to solve larger social disintegration through lessons, posters, and programs aimed at promoting selected values and virtues. Some, like respect for authority and promptness, seem more about behaving ourselves than about enhancing the character of democracy (Lockwood 1985/1986). But others, such as trustworthiness, diligence, and responsibility, are certainly necessary for sustaining communities of collaboration. In a democratic culture and curriculum, these affective dimensions of education are embedded in the ongoing process and content of the classroom community (Beane 1990a). A separate program or script of lessons is not necessary. Rather than being "taught" through contrived lessons or moralizing stories, "character" comes to life as people work together to research and solve problems, negotiate ideas, create projects, make decisions, and organize their efforts. As for examples of ethical dilemmas, there are plenty available, inside and outside the school, without having to make any up. And it is these kinds of real dilemmas, rather than those in fables or fairy tales, that offer the substance of inquiry in a democracy.

Curriculum and Culture

In the previous chapter, I suggested ways in which we might want to think about the curriculum if we want to teach the democratic way. Those included such things as organizing the curriculum around personal and social issues, integrating knowledge into the context of those themes, using more projects, emphasizing more authentic and reflective assessment, and placing a premium on group activities. I want to return to these ideas here as a way of suggesting that, sooner or later, thinking about curriculum this way is necessary for creating a democratic culture in the classroom.

Rhetoric about democratic schools has generally involved two good arguments. One is the insistence that to have democratic schools, all young people must have equitable access to the best opportunities *and* outcomes the school has to offer, especially those young people who have historically been excluded on the basis of race, class, gender, or handicapping condition. In this way, the school may meet the principle that Amy Gutmann (1987, 45) calls "nondiscrimination," which guarantees people the right to an education that allows them to participate in political decisions that affect their lives. The other argument is that to have democratic schools, we must open up opportunities for students to have a say in school governance and, less frequently, the planning of classroom experiences. Both of these arguments are absolutely essential to the concept of democratic schools.

Far less frequently, however, is the curriculum seen as an arena for needed change in the move toward democratic schools. Perhaps this is because the calls for democratic schools are so often made by university authorities in whose image the usual separate-subject curriculum of the schools is formed. All we need, they might say, is more access to what's already there. Or perhaps the curriculum issue is avoided because nothing about schooling is more taken for granted than the idea that the knowledge students ought to have is all defined by and contained within the usual subject and skill areas. Certainly, that view is reinforced by everything from textbook publishers to testing categories to teaching certifications and licenses. Or maybe it is because people know by either experience or intuition that nothing is so risky as fooling with what people think the curriculum of a school is supposed to be. In fact, there is an old saying that "changing the usual curriculum is like trying to move a cemetery." Some curriculum reformers like to add, "because we have so much respect for the dead."

In the end, though, the standard separate-subject curriculum found in schools where things are done the usual way greatly restricts the possibility of democratic classroom communities. The separate-subject approach is necessarily teacher dominated, since the knowledge to be mastered lies outside the experience of the young, but is presumably held by or accessible to the teacher as an adult and as a professionally prepared educator. Knowledge is something to be acquired and collected by the young. Acquisition, in turn, is demonstrated by the ability to recall the knowledge when called upon.

The separate-subject curriculum also follows the classical tradition that defines the teacher as master and the student as novice or apprentice. The teacher is expected to completely control the setting and to evaluate and rank the students. In the separate-subject approach, status depends not only on one's personal acquisition of knowledge, but also on whether it is more or less than that of others. Moreover, decisions about what knowledge is to be disseminated are made almost entirely apart from the classrooms (and schools). Teachers are conduits for knowledge selected by others, while students are consumers and collectors of that knowledge as they prepare for the adult world in which it will supposedly become useful.

When we choose to move in the direction of the curriculum possibilities offered in the previous chapter, the culture of the classroom moves as well. When the curriculum begins to organize around personal and social issues, the classroom takes on an aura of authenticity. It is connected to issues and concerns that students know are significant. When knowledge is integrated into the context of those themes, it comes to life. As it is applied to issues, it has purpose and worth. When the curriculum emphasizes projects and authentic assessment, students take purposeful action. When students and teachers plan together and when reflective assessment is emphasized, students assume greater responsibility and power. And when a premium is placed on group activities, collaboration becomes a way of life for teachers and students.

Authenticity, personal and social significance, application of knowledge, purposeful action, shared power and responsibility, collaboration—these are all hallmarks of a democratic culture. Their presence is a sign that a democratic community is coming to life. Their absence is a sign that some other kind of community is at work, one in which things are done the usual way. Yet these can only be fully realized if the curriculum itself is included in our

> The thirteen years of submission and passivity customarily provided to young people by American schools is an exceedingly poor preparation for resourceful, self-initiating problem solvers, not to mention free and critical citizens.
> Harvey Daniels and Marilyn Bizar, 1998

thinking how to create a democratic culture in schools. Ensuring equitable access to the best opportunities and outcomes the school has to offer gets us part of the way. Inviting students to have a say in governance does, too. But students and teachers do not come together for random reasons. They are supposed to do something. That something is the curriculum. Since the curriculum forms the basis of their roles and relationships, the culture of the classroom cannot change in any significant way if the curriculum does not. And if the curriculum does not change, whatever moves might have been made toward a democratic culture in other aspects of the school will eventually erode, as the usual way of doing curriculum eventually becomes the usual way of doing everything else.

At the End of the Day

There are many things about the usual way things are done in schools and classrooms that need to be transformed if we are to meet our obligation to teach the democratic way (see Figure 3–2). And we can change them if we really want to. We can work with our young people to create school governance and structures that befit a democratic society. We can be more respectful of the dignity of young people as well as the diversity among them. We can share power with young people and build more collaborative relationships with them. We can do these things if we really want to teach the democratic way.

For those teachers who are on this path, certain questions recur in their professional reflections.

- Do I see my classroom as a community or simply a collection of individuals? Do we work collaboratively? Do students participate in governing and maintaining the community?
- Do I see young people simply as students, or do I try to understand them as whole persons? Is their agenda evident in the agenda of the classroom? Do I take them seriously as people?
- Do I think of the diversity among students as a problem to overcome or as an asset to the potential richness of the classroom community? Are varieties of cultures evident in the

Figure 3–2

Suggestions for Getting Started

The Carnegie Corporation and the Center for Information and Research on Civic Learning and Engagement (2003) have suggested a number of ways in which we might begin. Naming the schools an "important venue for civic education," their report describes six promising approaches and explains each as follows:

1. Provide instruction in government, history, law, and democracy. Formal instruction in U.S. government, history, and democracy increases civic knowledge. This is a valuable goal in itself and may also contribute to young people's tendency to engage in civic and political activities over the long term. However, schools should avoid teaching only rote facts about dry procedures, which is unlikely to benefit students and may actually alienate them from politics.

2. Incorporate discussion of current local, national, and international issues and events into the classroom, particularly those that young people view as important to their lives. When young people have opportunities to discuss current issues in a classroom setting, they tend to have greater interest in politics, improved critical thinking and communications skills, more civic knowledge, and more interest in discussing public affairs out of school. Conversations, however, should be carefully moderated so that students feel welcome to speak from a variety of perspectives. Teachers need support in broaching controversial issues in classrooms since they may risk criticism or sanctions if they do so.

3. Design and implement programs that provide students with the opportunity to apply what they learn through performing community service that is linked to the formal curriculum and classroom instruction. Service programs are now common in K–12 schools. The ones that best develop engaged citizens are linked to the curriculum; consciously pursue civic outcomes, rather than seek only

---

(continues on next page)

to improve academic performance or to promote higher self-esteem; allow students to engage in meaningful work on serious public issues; give students a role in choosing and designing their projects; provide students with opportunities to reflect on the service work; allow students—especially older ones—to pursue political responses to problems consistent with laws that require public schools to be nonpartisan; and see service-learning as part of a broader philosophy toward education, not just a program that is adopted for a finite period in a particular course.

4. Offer extracurricular activities that provide opportunities for young people to get involved in their schools or communities. Long term studies of Americans show that those who participate in extracurricular activities in high school remain more civically engaged than their contemporaries even decades later. Thus, everyone should have opportunities to join high school groups, and such participation should be valued.

5. Encourage student participation in school governance. A long tradition of research suggests [those who] participate in the management of their own classrooms and schools build their civic skills and attitudes. Thus, giving students a voice in school governance is a promising way to encourage all young people to engage civically.

6. Encourage students' participation in simulations of democratic processes and procedures. Recent evidence indicates that simulations of voting, trials, legislative deliberation, and diplomacy in schools can lead to heightened political knowledge and interest.

Figure 3–2. *Continued*

curriculum, the structures, and the aesthetics of our classroom? Does the particular culture to which I belong dominate the classroom, or is it one among many that are evident?

■ Is our classroom a "court of knowledge"? Do we ask lots of questions about things? Do we search for explanations behind events, issues, and ideas? Do we access a wide variety

of resources in search of wide-ranging opinions and ideas?
Do we consider the ethics of situations, issues, and events?

- Am I considering only structures like grouping and governance in moving toward a democratic classroom, or am I
also working toward a democratic curriculum?

Questions like these are never fully resolved and require constant reflection because democracy is never a finished work. Moreover, the usual way of doing things is deeply entrenched in the
experiences and thinking of almost anyone who has attended
schools—and of course that is almost everyone. The tendency to
lean in that direction is strong, and the pull to return for those
who venture away is even more so. Resisting the pull is not an easy
thing to do. But for those who choose to teach the democratic way,
the pull toward a culture of respect, collaboration, diversity, and
inquiry is even stronger. And it is that pull and the exhilaration of
working in a democratic community that sustains them.

4 Being a Democratic Teacher

Teaching the democratic way involves constant reflection about the meaning of democracy and how it might be brought to life in the classroom. It also involves a considerable amount of courage and creativity in schools where things are otherwise done the usual way. What does it mean to be a democratic teacher? What leads teachers to teach this way? What do they think about? How do they sustain themselves and their work when so many things stand in the way of democratic practices in the school? These are extremely important questions, since the core of democratic teaching seems so often to lie not only within classroom culture and practices but also within the person who is the democratic teacher.

Through the Eyes of a Democratic Teacher

All too frequently, teachers who advocate for the democratic way are imagined as a certain stereotype: They are young, dress informally, have unkempt hair, wear sandals, ride bicycles to work, shop at health food stores, only watch public television, and always insist that students call them by their first names. While that may describe some democratic teachers, it hardly describes them all. Most often, though, that stereotype is used by critics of the democratic way to create the impression that advocates for the democratic way are somehow outside what is taken to be the mainstream of society. They are, of course, quite wrong. I have met teachers who would actually fit that description who have been tightly locked into very nondemocratic approaches once inside their classrooms. What's more, I clearly recall the first avid and outspoken advocate for democratic teaching I met. I still picture him standing up at faculty meetings criticizing the school bureaucracy, speaking out for student and teacher rights, and insisting we do something about the lack of social issues in the curriculum. He was an older teacher, nearing retirement, wearing a suit and tie, and known for his demanding teaching style. To this day, he reminds me that democratic teachers are defined by their beliefs and their practices, and definitely not by how they look. Given that, how might we know a democratic teacher if we met one? And if I wanted to head in that direction, what would be on my mind?

To begin with, democratic teachers seem to have certain beliefs about the young people they work with, whether small children or older adolescents. For these teachers, young people are not just students. They are real and whole people living real lives in a very real world, of which school is one piece. They are citizens of the society and the world with democratic rights for themselves and social obligations to the common good. They are entitled to have a say and to have their say taken seriously. They are entitled to be treated with dignity and respect. They are entitled to be called by their given names, respected in and for their diversity, and engaged in socially significant work. They have a right to ask questions, to have access to information and ideas, and to think carefully and critically about what they find out.

> If we educators love children so much, giving them engaging activities in the classroom is not enough; we also need to fight racism, poverty, and anything else that crushes their lives and spirits.
>
> Conrad Toepfer, ca. 1969

Democratic teachers also believe that young people are intelligent and thus have high expectations for their capacity to live and learn democratically rather than in the usual ways. They want young people to try out ideas rather than simply accepting what they read or hear from so-called experts. Moreover, they are not afraid of new knowledge, controversial issues, or questions to which they themselves do not already know the answer. In fact, many I have met seem only to ask questions to which they do not know the answer. For them, questions like *What do you think* is happening in the story? or *What do you think* the answer is? are very different from What is happening? or What is the answer? And they really do mean to have their students *think*. Parker Palmer is right when he claims that a great deal of what we do as teachers is rooted in the fears we carry with us into the classroom: fear of silence, fear of unpopularity, fear of losing control, fear that a bad lesson makes us a bad person. He goes on to say, though, that we "need not teach from a fearful place . . . if [we are] willing to stand someplace else in [our] inner landscape" (1998, 57). Democracy speaks the language of possibility and the politics of hope. When we choose to teach the democratic way, we are teaching from our hopes, not our fears—our hopes for more justice, more equity, more community, and more respect for human dignity.

Democratic teachers seem to constantly ask inquiring questions. They want to know all about who their students are, what they are concerned about, what they believe, what is on their agendas, and what they hope for. Democratic teachers also seem to live fully in the world, inquiring into politics and current events inside and outside the school and discussing events of the day with their students. They seem to understand more than other teachers that the school and the lives of young people are not isolated from the rest of the world.

Democratic teachers use a critical eye as they inquire into the world. They seem to always be looking behind the scene, asking why things are the way they are. They want to know why the curriculum is the way it is, who decided about mandated curriculum content or textbooks, and which school policies are inequitable. And they are not afraid of such questions because they realize that democracy is transparent. Critics and colleagues are sometimes driven to distraction by these kinds of critical questions and also by the fact that democratic teachers seem to insist that everyone reflect about the meaning of things and their consequences. Democratic teachers often seem to slow things down because they want to think and talk about how teaching methods work and whether policies are fair and why students and parents ought to have a voice in decisions.

Democratic teachers can often be identified by their over-involvement in things. They seem to volunteer for too many committees, sign up for too many conferences, and join too many groups. It goes without saying that teaching is an exhausting profession no matter how it is done. In a sense, teachers choose which path to take toward the inevitable exhaustion. Democratic teachers know that advocating for the democratic way requires participation and involvement. It cannot be done from the sidelines. On the other hand, I have met just as many teachers who seem exhausted not by too much participation, but by having to live with decisions made by committees they did not sign up for.

> *Democratic teachers teach from hope. They bring their hearts to school.*
> Ken Bergstrom, ca. 1993

In the end, though, democratic teachers are perhaps best known for standing up for young people and democracy. In faculty room conversations, committee meetings, staff meetings, and even casual hallway conversations, they seem never to let go of their compassion for the young or their concern for the democratic way. They speak for equity and justice in school policies and procedures, for fuller participation in decision making, for greater attention to cultural diversity, and for the rights and interests of students as well as parents who can't or don't know how to speak for their children. In schools where the usual way of doing things is deeply entrenched, taking such stands can make democratic teachers very unpopular. Their critics sometimes think they are simply against everything. Faced with the usual way of doing things, that is partially true—but only because they are for the democratic way.

Living in a Democratic Community

Up to this point, I have concentrated on the teacher as an individual professional who chooses to teach the democratic way. Inviting and ethical as the democratic way may be, it is also very difficult to sustain, especially if one is following this path alone in a school that insists on doing things the usual way. It is possible to go it alone, but the frustration of trying to be democratic in an undemocratic situation, as well as the almost certain criticism from cynical colleagues, administrators, and others, takes a huge emotional toll. I know many teachers like this who end up moving from school to school in search of like-minded colleagues or who leave teaching altogether. So while the move toward teaching the democratic way may begin with an individual teacher, it is in the best interest of that person and the idea itself to work toward creating a democratic professional community in the school. How might this begin? What kinds of things might a group of professionals do to build and sustain a democratic community? (See Figure 4–1.)

As we have already seen, a democratic community is one in which people come together to address shared concerns using democratic processes. For teachers, this partly means addressing concerns about their professional lives and work, including negotiating working conditions and school structures. Our focus here, however, will be on curriculum, teaching, school culture and climate, and other aspects of school life. In this regard, there are many ways teachers might come together as a democratic professional community. But it is not just the fact that the teachers come together that marks a democratic professional community; it is also what they do.

One of the best examples is teacher research groups. Introduced in schools in the 194? teacher research groups were intended as a forum for tea   s to work together to resolve school problems. Unlike the   al committee format, research groups systematically gather a   alyze data to inform decisions about various problems or is   s. For example, suppose we wanted to increase parent partic   ation in school events. A typical committee format would bring together some teachers and administrators, and perhaps a parent, to brainstorm some ideas. After discussion, one or two ideas would be selected and implemented during the year. In an action research forum, such issues would be treated quite differently. A group of teachers might begin by inviting some parents and students to join them in searching for ideas. Once formed, the group raises pertinent questions, like Why do some parents participate while other don't? or What barriers do parents think prevent them for participating? Guided by such questions the group gathers information from a sample of parents through surveys, interviews, and focus groups.

Figure 4–1

Sources for Help in Getting Started

Teachers and other educators getting started toward teaching the democratic way can access a variety of helpful resources. Here are some examples.

Organizations

Among the many groups and organizations, large and small, that advocate for democratic education, these six are especially focused on that mission.

Rethinking Schools. The most prominent grassroots collective of educators advocating for democracy in education, Rethinking Schools publishes a journal and books on timely topics and remains closely tied to the well-known Milwaukee bilingual school La Escuela Fratney. To subscribe to the quarterly *Rethinking Schools* magazine, order Rethinking Schools books, or read past articles, visit www.rethinkingschools.org.

Institute for Democracy in Education. Housed at Ohio University, Athens, OH, the institute publishes the journal *Democracy and Education*, organizes an annual conference, and sponsors a network of over twenty regional centers. Find IDE at www.ohiou.edu/ide.

Teaching Tolerance. A project of the Southern Poverty Law Center, Teaching Tolerance has been supporting educational efforts to promote respect for differences and an appreciation of diversity since 1991. Teaching Tolerance publishes a free semiannual magazine that profiles educators, schools, and programs promoting diversity and equity. In addition, the program produces and distributes free, high-quality antibias multimedia kits. Current and back issues of the magazine, useful activities and resources, and grant information are available on the project's website at www.teachingtolerance.org.

Educators for Social Responsibility. A prominent and long-standing organization, ESR advocates for democratic

---

(*continues on next page*)

education through a variety of publications, school programs, conferences, and other supports. ESR can be found at www.esrnational.org.

League of Professional Schools. Housed at the University of Georgia, LPS sponsors a network of schools promoting democratic governance and learning. The league offers school conferences, site facilitation, materials, and other supports. Find LPS at www.coe.uga/lps.

National Service-Learning Clearinghouse. The clearinghouse is a tremendous resource for information on this aspect of democratic education, with information about projects, publications, conferences, and other resources. The clearinghouse is found at www.servicelearning.org.

Books
Among the many books and other print materials advocating for democratic education, these five consist mainly of essays written by educators in schools.

Allen, J., ed. 1999. *Class Actions: Teaching for Social Justice in Elementary and Middle School.* New York: Teachers College Press.

Apple, M. W., and J. A. Beane, eds. 1995. *Democratic Schools.* Alexandria, VA: Association for Supervision and Curriculum Development.

Beyer, L. E., ed. 1996. *Creating Democratic Classrooms: The Struggle to Integrate Theory and Practice.* New York: Teachers College Press.

Hall, I., C. Campbell, and E. Miech, eds. 1997. *Class Acts: Teachers Reflect on Their Own Classroom Practice.* Cambridge, MA: Harvard University Press.

McDermott, C., ed. 1998. *Beyond the Silence: Listening for Democracy.* Portsmouth, NH: Heinemann.

Figure 4–1. *Continued*

They also consult with other schools and search out research on parent participation. These data are then analyzed and discussed with an eye to what parents themselves say about their participation in school events. Recommendations for how to improve participation are based on the data gathered and once implemented are evaluated through follow-up interviews or surveys.

In a variation of that process, teacher research is frequently carried out in groups in which each teacher has a different topic. In this case, the questions and concerns may vary widely among the group as teachers inquire into problems and issues in their own classrooms. Working as individuals, the teachers clarify their own questions and concerns, figure out how to gather data, work through the project, and are supported and encouraged by the group. While the impact on whole-school policies may not be as immediate and direct as when the whole group owns one major issue, this second approach has its own kind of power. As teachers come to know each other's professional questions, support each other through their projects, and learn about each other's results, the kind of mutual respect and concern crucial to democratic living is almost always a result.

Again, though, if simply coming together in a group were enough to build and sustain a democratic professional community, the schools would by now be overflowing with democracy. After all, meetings and committees are a staple of school life for teachers, albeit not always a pleasant one. Too often, these are settings for personal agendas, endless discussions, and ignored or forgotten recommendations—hardly a portrait of a democratic community. At some point, decisions made at higher levels and handed down seem a relief from the drudgery of committee meetings. In the case of teacher action research, however, the identification of questions to be addressed, the systematic gathering of data, and the power of informed decision making offer a greater chance for meaningful work and action.

Just as important, the very idea of teacher action research is a lesson in the democratic way of doing things. While educational research has historically been owned and handed down by academic researchers external to the schools, action research places ownership in the hands of those within the school. When teachers are in a position to name important research questions and when they are seen as capable of conducting their own inquiries, educational research itself is democratized. And in that sense, teacher action research is one of the surest ways to move beyond the individual democratic teacher toward a democratic professional community.

Another way in which teachers might come together as a professional democratic community is through teacher study groups. In this setting, small groups of teachers select books, journal articles, and other professional media to guide their discussion of significant topics or issues. Michael DePung (2001) describes an excellent case study of a teacher study group that emerged from efforts by him and other young teachers to create a sense of community at their school. The focus of DePung's study group was the book *Methods That Matter: Six Structures for Best Practice Classrooms* (Daniels and Bizar 1998). The group met biweekly to discuss various chapters and their attempts to implement ideas from them. Importantly, the structures addressed in the book are themselves exactly the kinds of practices that are associated with democratic classrooms: integrative units, small-group activities, representing-to-learn, classroom workshops, authentic experiences, and reflective assessment. The study group's mix of discussion, classroom implementation, journaling, and mutual classroom observations led to considerable professional development in the school and participation by nearly two-thirds of the faculty. Most telling, though, is DePung's observation:

> [Teachers] must experience that democratic process that their students would experience, and if they are to work in harmony and enjoy that work and pass such an attitude on to students, then they must also have a vested interest in the school culture—beyond their tenure and retirement packages. (2001, 18)

We know that the best way for young people to learn the democratic way is to live it. DePung reminds us that the same is true for teachers. That should tell us something about the self-defeating nature of the usual way of doing things.

Action research and teacher study groups are two arrangements with explicit potential for creating a democratic professional community in a school. Other possibilities are already available in many schools, though they are not often thought of in terms of doing things the democratic way. The most obvious example is teaching teams, long popular in elementary and middle schools and beginning to take hold in many high schools. The fact is that teams have most often become a forum for small groups of teachers to constantly discuss ways of refining classroom management and discipline for the students they share. Lost in this view is the idea that the teaming concept was meant to put in the hands of teachers decisions about curriculum, scheduling, grouping, and other matters that had historically been made by administrators. Taken this way, teaming would be one response to DePung's admonition that teachers have opportunities to experience the kind of democracy their students should. Granted, teachers are often put into teams without planning time and other supports necessary for their work. But again, even when those supports are in place, the dominant theme of team discussions is student control (Shaw 1993).

What would teams work on if they could see themselves as an opportunity for democratic community? They would likely spend more time sharing philosophies about teaching, creating arrangements for curriculum collaboration, or discussing possibilities for community building with their students. And certainly they would constantly look for ways in which students might collaborate with them through student advisory committees, reflective assessments of team activities, and other participatory arrangements. In this sense, teaming is a good example of an important rule of thumb. To move toward a democratic professional community, we do not always have to add on new structures. In fact, the best place to start may well be by looking at current school structures and asking whether any of them could contribute if only they were thought of in a democratic way.

If a democratic professional community is to be created and sustained, democratic participation must sooner or later be extended into decision making about all areas of school life. A democratic culture is created out of a shared vision, and unless people have a say in things, they are simply not very likely to see themselves as part of that vision. One very good example of how this might look is built into several prominent models for comprehensive school reform. Schools are encouraged to form a leadership team consisting of teachers, administrators, and others who oversee implementation of a school reform model. Over time, this group is responsible for planning professional development, addressing emerging school issues, assessing progress of the school, and more. And while the decisions the group makes are important from the outset, even more important is the potential for sustaining serious reform as more people share in deciding how it will happen. Ann Yehle, a Midwest principal, said this well in a talk to the school faculty as the year opened:

> There was a time when things weren't so good at our school. But we came together. And coming together was our beginning, staying together these last few years has led to progress, and now, really working together will be our success. And our student's success. Am I hoping, am I dreaming? Perhaps, but not if we hope the same hope and dream the same dream.

Not surprisingly, in his study of several democratic schools, George Wood (1992) reports this kind of shared governance as a common feature among them. One of the most prominent examples is La Escuela Fratney/Fratney School in Milwaukee, Wisconsin (Peterson 1995). The school's council of parents and teachers makes virtually all policy decisions as well as addressing problems and concerns emerging from both parents and professionals regarding everything from homework to parent involvement to support for new teachers. In citing these examples of schoolwide governance, it may seem that I have moved away from the democratic teacher and classroom. But when the democratic way defines the culture of a school, the teachers within need no longer feel as though they are always swimming upstream in teaching the democratic way in their own classrooms.

In this regard, La Escuela Fratney/Fratney School has yet another lesson for us, for the school did not suddenly appear out of nowhere ready to take in teachers who wanted to teach the democratic way. Rather it came into being as a result of democratic educators creating a professional community. There have been many such groups, formal and informal, formed over the years all around the country: The Institute for Democracy in Education in Ohio, the Boston Women Teachers Group, the Public Education Information Network in St. Louis, the League of Professional Schools, and Educators for Social Responsibility. Perhaps the most widely known among them all is Rethinking Schools, the community of educators and citizens in Milwaukee, out of which emerged the well-known journal of the same name, the school known as La Escuela Fratney, and wonderful publications such as *The New Teacher Handbook* (Rethinking Schools 2004). Bob Peterson, a founding member, tells the story this way.

Rethinking Schools was founded in 1986 by teachers, parents, and community activists who were feeling powerless in the face of an unresponsive school board and news media that refused to deal with educational issues in depth. It grew out of discussions in a small book study group of about a dozen people, some of whom had been active in different movements for social justice.

Using a rickety Apple IIe computer and a kitchen table pressed into service as a layout board, we assembled the first issue of our quarterly journal, *Rethinking Schools*, with the ambitious goal of fundamentally altering the educational debate in our community. Using a tabloid format, printed on inexpensive newsprint, we passed out the first issue at the local union meeting and at as many schools as we could. The Rethinking Schools group acted as an editorial board, a critical lens through which to analyze our own teaching, a personal support group, and a network to engage in political action.

We discovered that in analyzing the racial and class inequities in Milwaukee schools and proposing antiracist, activist solutions, grounded in a broad vision of social justice, we began to reach a national audience. With some variation, we found that local problems were national problems. Rethinking Schools began to give education activists around the country the sense that we were part of a broader movement that linked school change with social change.

From the beginning we set ourselves a mission that involved delicate balancing acts: to defend the principle of public education as we propose its massive overhaul; to insist that schools can make a huge difference in children's lives, even as we highlight what schools can't do without more profound social and economic changes; to stay grounded and practical without extinguishing the utopian dreams that nourish our activism. These tensions have animated every issue of the journal.

Two essential commitments keep us focused: our embrace of the movement for racial justice and our classroom-eye view of school issues. Historically, antiracism has been a vital engine of justice in America. If history teaches anything, it's that without race at the center no meaningful change is possible. As a multi-racial collective, we consistently draw on our insights gleaned from participation in struggles for racial justice to analyze everything from children's literature to tracking to patterns of school funding. This orientation continues to be a compass for Rethinking Schools' direction.

Second, we are not policy wonks closeted in office buildings, thinking up grandiose, top-down school reform models. We are mostly teachers, as we have been from the very start of the Rethinking Schools project, and we imagine change from the grassroots, from the classroom on up. Through articles and our books *Rethinking Columbus, Rethinking Our Classrooms*—volumes 1 and 2, *Reading, Writing and Rising Up*, and *Rethinking Globalization*, we've sought to offer educators models of critical, multicultural teaching, grounded in story and concrete example. In these and other publications we have consistently maintained that schools can re-name, restructure and re-organize all they want, but unless they also attend to what transpires between student and teacher, reform plans are doomed to fail.

Though democratic communities of professional colleagues are usually easier to start than to sustain, the story of Rethinking Schools tells us that all things are possible. Teachers lead very busy lives, and those who teach the democratic way are no excep-

Rethinking Schools and similar groups are an important voice in keeping democratic education alive.

tion. But going it completely alone is difficult and, in some sense, unnecessary. Teachers who begin to teach the democratic way can usually find like-minded colleagues if they look around, and just as often they are found by others who are looking as well.

Graduate School the Democratic Way

Any university professor who advocates for progressive and democratic education will soon be asked what should be done to make teacher education that way. This is a fair question. Not only should advocates put their money where their mouths are, but also, given the complications of democratic education, it is unfair to tell teachers to follow that road unless professors are walking it themselves. Ironically, though, as popular as the rhetoric of democratic education is among professors, its reality in teacher education programs is rare. Among the exceptions is the program at Evergreen State College in Olympia, Washington, and Michael Varvus' (2002) account describes how teacher education for democracy might actually look. At the same time, the struggle to put it in place suggests that such work is definitely not for the fainthearted or marginally committed. Imagine, for example, what it means to create teacher education programs whose aims, as Landon Beyer (1996, 10) says, are "creating educational practices aimed at social justice rather than stability, participation rather than silencing and exclusion, liberation rather than domination, equity rather than exploitation."

But I have saved for last the one example of a possible democratic community that has historically seemed most hopeless for advocates of the democratic way—graduate degree programs for teachers. As deeply rooted as the "usual" way of doing things is in schools, that way is a model of flexibility compared with what we see in graduate schools of education. The scheduling of courses, the disinterest in teachers' knowledge and experience, the distance of many professors from the life of schools, and the topics that are featured all sometimes seemed designed to turn teachers away rather than to invite them in. This is not to say that topics or courses typically found in graduate schools of education are of no importance, nor am I trying to be anti-intellectual. But it is hard to deny that the typical graduate education course does little to promote democracy beyond talking about it, as many actually do. But if talking about democratic teaching in graduate education classes were enough, the schools would look a lot different than they do now.

What might a graduate education program look like if it were designed to teach the democratic way? I want to describe one example here. I'm not saying it's the only example, but it does open the door for thinking about what such a program might look like and what questions it might raise.

Picture a group of fifteen or so teachers beginning their master's degree program. They are a diverse group, representing a variety of grade levels and teaching areas. The setting is a classroom in a school located near where everyone teaches. It will be used as a home base for their weekly four-hour meetings. These teachers will spend nearly two years together in a cohort group with a university core instructor assigned to them the whole time. The program they have enrolled in is meant to be a democratic experience. Among other things, this means that teachers are considered professional adults capable of identifying the direction for their own professional development; moreover, their experiences and knowledge regarding education are considered at least as valuable as those held by professors or within education textbooks. So instead of working from a preset syllabus, the group must make some plans for itself.

Early on, the teachers identify, as individuals, questions about their own teaching, the young people they work with, the schools they are in, and their colleagues, as well as other questions about education or schooling in general. Small groups are formed to look for common, shared questions, which are clustered into topics or themes. Then the small groups share their themes and a common list for the whole group is created. These themes and the questions within them will become the organizing centers for much of the group's work in the program.

Several themes emerge in this particular group. Questions about children in their own classrooms combine with general questions about how children think and learn to form a theme they name "All My Children." Questions about their own working conditions and colleagues combine with general questions about the public perceptions of the teaching profession to form the theme "Days of Our Lives." Questions about children's lives outside the schools along with questions about poverty, racism, and other conditions combine to form the theme "As the World Turns." And questions about purposes of schools, curriculum mandates, and the best teaching methods combine to form "The Guiding Light."

The group decides to begin with "All My Children." Looking at the questions that formed the theme, they create some possible activities to answer each question. They decide to interview three or four young people in each of their classes and share the results. A few add to that by also interviewing the parents of their students, while others choose to talk to guidance counselors and social workers. They also decide to share samples of their students' work for group discussion. Forming small groups according to decades in which they were born, they create a timeline of childhood and adolescent experiences spanning over fifty years. In addition, they search for some readings related to their questions, including selections from the books they have chosen from the program list. With these and other activities, this theme will last about six to eight weeks. Then the group will go back to the theme list, choose another, and organize it in the same way.

In addition to work on the themes, each teacher will also carry out an extensive action research project while in the program. This project will focus on some particular question or issue related to his or her own teaching. Where two or more teachers have the same question or issue, they might choose to do a collaborative project. In this group, topics for projects include integrating the first-grade curriculum around environmental issues, helping a low-income parent learn ways of supporting her children's language development, interviewing former students to see what they remember about high school, and thinking through the debates over didactic and constructivist math (a small-group project). As the projects evolve, small groups meet to give feedback and support. Toward the end of the program, the teachers share their projects with the whole group as well as with colleagues at their home schools.

> *Teachers can lead the way by making democracy the guiding philosophy in our schools, and by giving it the opportunity of working itself out in real life situations.*
> Charles Wesley, 1941

Over the course of three or four months during their time together, the group will also spend one evening in the classroom of each member. For part of that evening, the host teacher will conduct a school tour, talk about his or her curriculum and teaching, and have the group try out one or two activities that the host teacher uses with his or her students. Lively discussions ensue as members of the group share ideas and compare teaching styles, curriculum ideas, and school cultures. This is also a time when the teachers swap materials they have found helpful with their students. Once all the visits have been completed, the group will reflect on similarities and differences in teaching styles, curriculum preferences, school designs and resources, and whatever else they have observed during their visits.

As the end of the group's program nears, they take time over several weeks to reflect on what they have done together. They search through files, journals, handouts, schedules, and other artifacts to reconstruct various themes and activities, which are placed on a timeline. Self and group evaluations are prepared and become the content for discussions about what did and did not seem to go well, what was most or least helpful, and how the group worked together.

In their evaluations of the program, the teachers speak in positive terms about their personal and professional experiences in the group. They appreciate the recognition of their professional knowledge, the fact that they have a large say in what happens, the chance to see other schools and classrooms, the pertinence of the themes to their professional lives, and the importance of what they learn about themselves and their topic as they complete the action research project. But mostly they talk about how much they appreciate being part of "the group" as a professional community where they can share ideas, debate issues, and expand their sense of professional identity.

For a number of years, I taught in just such a program at the National College of Education at National-Louis University. While various instructors organized groups differently, all shared a common conceptual framework promoting democratic education and social justice. Among the guiding ideas generally shared among faculty were the following:

- Teachers' experiences are important sources for understanding education, at least as important as those of university instructors or textbook authors.

- As professional adults, teachers are capable of identifying important directions for their own development.
- Each group of teachers is unique in many ways, and thus the curriculum will vary across groups.
- Each group needs to plan its own program given its own sense of needs, interests, problems, and concerns.
- Issues about group dynamics or procedures are determined by the group rather than by the instructor or other university personnel.
- Matters having to do with assessment of projects and other work as well as evaluation of group experiences and instructor contributions should be the responsibility of the group.
- Rather than using the course strands of the program to organize the curriculum, they are integrated into themes relevant to the teachers' lives and work.
- Logistical matters such as scheduling, meeting site, and so on, are determined by the group.

Obviously, these kinds of practices, inspired by democratic principles, are quite different from most graduate programs for teachers. The tremendous popularity of the program among teachers, aside from the usual goal of pay raises, was in many ways an indication of how attractive and powerful such principles can be. But living up to those principles in the real life of the group proved challenging for both teachers and university instructors alike.

Before enrolling in the program, teachers were involved in various information sessions, were given materials to read, and typically heard stories from colleagues who had been in previous groups. They enrolled because it sounded good to them, or at least better than more traditional alternatives. But hearing about the program and going through it often proved to be two different things. Like almost everyone else's experience, teachers' own experiences in school and college have generally been in authoritarian, textbook-driven, passive settings. Now they were suddenly in a setting where they had to make decisions for themselves as individuals and as a group. The core instructor was willing to facilitate, but deliberately tried to wait for the individual or group to make decisions.

Many teachers struggled with this shift in power relations. Paid to make curriculum decisions with children by day, they seemed paralyzed to do the same in their own graduate program at night. Faced with a lack of stringent, predetermined assessment criteria, they frequently floundered when thinking about creating their own and sometimes even demanded that the core instructor do that for them. Even decisions about what time to break for dinner could be painful. And who could blame the teachers? Where would they have learned to do these things? And why wouldn't they be suspicious right to the end that someone would pull the rug out from under them and veto their decisions?

To their credit, however, almost all groups found their way in the midst of this democratic ambiguity. Over time, messy beginnings evolved into conscious democratic group cultures complete with situational leaders; consistent rules for making decisions; familiar ways of solving problems; patterns of activities that reflected the group's preferred learning style; and, of course, continuing issues over interpersonal dynamics and conflicting values. For a few teachers and the occasional group, that portrait never really materialized. Not surprisingly, the path to program completion in these cases was marked by the search for shortcuts, work avoidance, tardiness, and the invention of ways to stay away from deeper discussion. In some ways, these cases seemed more like the typical graduate school and, I would maintain, offered no less by way of teacher education. But they also served as reminders of how difficult democracy can be and how people may choose to avoid its challenges or take advantage of the lack of authoritarian rules.

For the core instructors, the challenges of democratic living could be just as daunting. These people, too, had usually experienced schooling as an authoritarian affair, including the typical graduate school, where teacher knowledge was not necessarily valued. They, too, were used to lectures, textbook assignments, and papers meant to please professors. Now they were confronted with difficult questions: How should the group plan together? When do I intervene and when do I keep silent? What is my role in the group? How do I prepare when the group has not decided on a direction? How long do I wait for the group to make a decision? How do I disagree with someone in the group without devaluing his or her idea or unfairly using my power as the appointed instructor? What if I disagree with a teacher's action research topic? Do I go ahead with a group decision even if previous experience tells me it might not be a good one? If some of the group members avoid responsibility, do I say something, or is that their right? And if I say something, does that imply to the rest of the group that I had hidden rules all along?

> *The solution to the messiness of democracy is more of it—and more time set aside to make it work.*
> Deborah Meier, 2004

Even for those of us who like to think of ourselves as democratic and progressive educators, these are extremely difficult questions. Talking about democracy is one thing. Sitting in a group of teachers expecting it to is quite another. I recall many times driving home at night after a group meeting wondering if someone had agreed with me on principle or because I was the designated instructor. I can't even begin to count the number of times individuals or groups would simply say, "You decide," and how tempting that could be. And I had not been in the program long when I discovered that my favorite educational readings were not similarly admired by most teachers. Yet in the midst of those struggles, a number of important lessons emerged about democratic education, especially as it relates to teachers and their own professional development. Some of those lessons were affirming, others were hard to learn.

Teaching democratically means turning the floor over to the group. For the core instructor, this means letting go of the idea that "I know what the group needs and my job is to see that they get it." In some ways, I found this to be very liberating. No longer was I responsible for the risky business of deciding what the group should do and how they should do it. Instead, I found myself inside the group, looking like everyone else for a place and a role and wondering what contributions to make. Yet this also meant sometimes watching a group make a decision to do something that previous groups had tried and regretted. Avoiding the temptation to intervene was not always easy, but I came to learn that democratic learning communities must have a chance to find their own way or risk losing their sense of power.

Announcing an intention to be "democratic" sets the core instructor up for constant scrutiny. The group now expects to make decisions for itself and to have those decisions honored. Should I stray from democratic procedure, the group is sure to issue a quick reminder: "We thought this was supposed to be a democratic group!" Thus, I had to understand that once democracy is announced, whatever I might subsequently want must be put up for group consideration. Happily, stepping back in this way made it possible to learn that what teachers see as their needs and issues was usually more interesting, challenging, and meaningful than what I would have had in mind for them.

What teachers think about and want to work on is almost always connected to larger policy issues and debates and occurs in the context of a complicated and largely unjust world. Finding better ways to help struggling students, responding to curriculum mandates, wondering how to deal with increasing job stress, figuring out how to improve family involvement—seriously exploring all of these involves understanding the school as a social institution with a complex and sometimes unsavory history. In this way, the larger policy issues that I might have brought to the group in an abstract way suddenly had a meaningful context. Now the teachers found talk about these issues interesting because it helped them think about their own work. In that context, the knowledge I brought to the group actually took on importance for the teachers. Even the often deadening history of education became important, as it was connected to the issues we had named.

Groups do not always want to take responsibility for making decisions or be burdened with the task of doing so. At these times, it is very easy to slip away from democratic deliberation. Thus, the instructor and the group have to understand that there is no turning back if we are serious about democracy. This can be especially hard for group members who have already put in a long day of intense work and sometimes just do not have the energy for more sustained effort. In the instructor's role, I learned it was better to postpone important decisions on such occasions than to make some that no one was really committed to. It was helpful to remember that this lost time was no worse than if the group had slept through a lecture in the usual graduate class.

Learning the ins and outs of democratic interaction in the context of group discussions is not easy. Early on, a teacher who had some experience with group dynamics plotted the flow of questions and comments in one of my groups for a few nights and suggested I look at it. To my embarrassment, the diagrams showed that the discussion flowed through me as I responded to each question and comment, sometimes after but usually before anyone else did. This was clearly a carryover from my days teaching in a typical graduate program and would prove to be a difficult habit to break. After several unsuccessful attempts, I finally had to keep a piece of paper in front of me that said, "Shut Up!" That sign allowed me to learn one of the great lessons of democratic teaching: No matter what idea or comment I wanted to express, if I waited long enough, someone else in the group would almost always say it. And if they didn't, I would eventually get my turn. Trying to shift power from the teacher to the group is very difficult, especially since most of us have had so little experience with it. Learning to do so requires considerable time and drastic action. Moreover, as long as the instructor is the original "designated leader," there will always be some tension over this matter.

The democratic classroom community looks just like groups in the larger society, even when the classroom group is made up of professional educators. Teachers bring to the group diverse experiences, knowledge, values, and expectations. For some individuals, exercising democratic control over their own agenda comes easily. For most it is a struggle that involves patience on their part as well as that of the designated instructor. And for a few in nearly every group, the lack of authoritarian control seems like an opportunity to avoid work and responsibility. This last group, small as it is, can create a dilemma for the entire group and for the designated instructor. Although the groups I worked with talked a good deal about how relieved they felt to be in a noncompetitive structure, some group members would eventually complain that the "slackers" were not doing as much work as they were and should be penalized through lesser grades or extra work—the same kind of penalties that so many teachers use when their own students seem to avoid work. I must admit that such reasoning seemed very tempting at times. Attempting to be a democratic teacher means dealing with your own past experiences as well as critics who question your professional rigor. In this context, it is hard not to take personally the actions of those who misuse the democratic opportunity, hard not to feel "walked on."

Eventually, I came to understand that intervening in a punitive way would suggest that democracy was only for those who chose to use it in a particular way and that the shift of power away from the instructor was conditional. Instead, I argued publicly that this is what democratic groups look like while simultaneously sending a signal to the individuals in question that I was not ignorant of their choices. But this issue was frequently on my mind as it is with so many teachers who try the democratic way. In a sense, moving in this direction does mean opening yourself up to being walked on. There may be many reasons why some individuals choose not to pull their weight in a group, from personal issues to difficulty with autonomy. But most would probably not have done any differently in a traditional program. Punishing them for not being prepared to participate in a democratic community is not a wise path to sustaining the democratic way.

Among all the difficulties of sustaining this attempt at democratic professional development, none was so persistent as the constant comparison with traditional graduate education programs. From subtle comments to public letters, detractors supplied an endless flow of complaints about the lack of "rigor," "content," and "structure" in the program. This took a serious toll on instructors and teacher/students alike. Sadly, the teachers in the group often came to doubt their professional competence and experience. Even as they talked about how much they were gaining personally and professionally, they also wondered if there was something more they should be doing. This was especially difficult when the critics were colleagues at their home schools who had gone through more traditional programs.

We talked openly about the criticism and loss of confidence. Intellectually, the teachers knew that the expectations here were higher than in a program where teachers were passive recipients of content chosen by professors. They knew that their action research projects were at least as rich and powerful as the narrow master's degree theses that line college library shelves. They knew the difference between intellectual rigor and jumping through academic hoops. All of these things they knew. But still they had lingering doubts.

With this steady stream of criticism as a constant reminder, a very painful lesson was made clear. The notion of the teacher as a nonthinking technician, incapable of learning from experience or creating new professional knowledge, is deeply rooted in the psyche of almost everyone in the profession, from professors and consultants to administrators to the teachers themselves. It is very hard for these people to accept an alternative notion, even when the evidence is right before them. Just as so many young people are treated as unthinking persons in their role as students, so are their teachers treated when it's time for professional development. For this reason, democratic professional development programs, especially in graduate schools of education, are not only rare, but—where they do exist—extremely fragile. And as good as these programs are, they never seem to be quite good enough to satisfy misguided critics on the outside or some doubtful participants on the inside. Clearly, the way in which authoritarian policies and experiences can erode self-confidence works as powerfully inside the profession as it does in the general society. And working to reclaim that confidence is part of teaching the democratic way.

At the End of the Day

The existence of that graduate program, complex as it was, speaks vividly to the possibilities of creating democratic communities. There, and especially in schools, such communities are crucial to sustaining the democratic way of teaching. If we who advocate for that kind of teaching want to keep our ideas alive, we need to think continuously together about questions like these:

- Who are we, and what do we believe about young people, our schools, our communities and cultures, and our obligations?
- Do we act in ways that invite other professionals to join us, or are we overly critical of colleagues?
- Do we always have to invent new ways to find community, or can we find within the schools already existing possibilities for doing so?
- If we are among those who supposedly "teach" teachers, can we say that we are really seeking to create more democratic spaces, or do we only talk about what teachers should do in their schools?

5 Sustaining the Democratic Way

Democracy is a timeless idea. For this reason, I have tried to avoid analyzing current education policies and politics in previous chapters in making the case for teaching the democratic way. The democratic way of doing things stands on its own merits, not on criticism of other ways. But if we are to think about how to sustain the democratic way, we must consider its prospects for the future. And that begins with a look at its current status.

Only a decade ago, we were in the midst of what seemed to be a renaissance of interest in ideas associated with teaching the democratic way. Around the country, educators were talking about interdisciplinary and integrative curriculum, detracking, problem-centered math and science, project-centered learning, and many more ideas like these. In many cases, these discussions were not simply about teaching methods, but about redirecting classrooms and schools toward more institutional equity, more meaningful learning, more culturally responsive content, more authentic assessments, and more socially conscious purposes. Conferences, journals, and workshops were full of these ideas, and more than a few teachers and schools created projects and programs to bring them to life.

Ironically, though, that renaissance of interest was surrounded by a steady growth in the power of social and economic conservatives who, as part of the rollback of everything public and progressive, were using legislative policy to move the schools in quite the opposite direction. In retrospect, it would be more than a little appropriate to say that the democratic impulse in the schools did not have a prayer in the face of what Michael Apple (1993) and others have dubbed the "Conservative Restoration." Today, the democratic educational ideas so popular just a decade ago have fallen on hard times, marginalized in public and professional media, their advocates silenced by the language of the new accountability movement and censored by the growing moral authority of standards and testing. For anyone advocating the democratic way, the title of Jonathan Kozol's 1975 book seems especially relevant today: *The Night Is Dark and I Am Far from Home*.

In dismantling democratic initiatives, advocates of the new accountability have set up a convenient rhetorical contrast: their supposedly "rigorous" standards and tests versus the allegedly "soft" methods of "progressive" and democratic initiatives (see, for example, Hirsch 1987; Ravitch 2000). According to this rhetoric, the quality of public education has been going steadily downhill since the 1960s. What is needed to make things right is a good dose of hard-nosed academic retrofitting. No matter, by the way, that the 1960s were actually a decade of some of the most conservative measures ever seen in education, including behavioral objectives, teaching machines, emphasis on structure of the disciplines, teacher-proof curriculum packages, and performance contracting for student achievement. What does matter is that to make the new accountability seem the road to salvation, democratic and progressive ideas must be made to seem the enemy of educational progress.

Meanwhile, educators and policy hopefuls who had shown such interest in democratic educational arrangements first let go of that interest to jump on the bandwagon of establishing subject standards for the curriculum. Whatever suspicions they may have had about standards were washed away one by one. For example, the cry for standards had emerged in the 1980s on the heels of *A*

Nation at Risk, a report in which ill-substantiated data were used to blame schools for this country's alleged loss of prominence in international economic competition (National Commission on Excellence in Education 1983). Though many educators found that report insulting, there was a certain appeal for some in the argument that academic standards would enhance "educational equity" by forcing bad schools to get better. And educator concerns about bureaucratic control eventually gave way to the standard-bearers' promises that they only wanted to "set" standards and had no intention whatsoever of telling local schools or teachers how to meet them.

On the same day in 1994 that Congress approved the idea of national standards, it defeated required "opportunity to learn" standards that would have ensured that teachers and students in our poorest schools would have the resources needed to meet the standards. Sadly, hardly anyone noticed, and the argument that standards would bring equity continued with little or no reference to the deteriorating conditions that override school improvement efforts in so many urban and rural communities. But as the new millennium approached, nagging questions began to surface: How can the economy be so good if the schools are so bad? and If all students achieve all standards at the highest level, will they all really get high-paying professional jobs? By then, however, what Marion Brady (2000) has called the "standards juggernaut" had gained a full head of steam.

There was an emerging paradox in all of this for many main-stream educators. The standards they had come to love, such as those developed by the National Council for Teachers of Mathematics and the National Council for Teachers of English, were being replaced by new state standards heavily influenced by conservative forces. In the end, standards that spoke to skills like problem solving or critical thinking or application, had mostly given way to longer and more detailed lists of subject-centered content items, phonics-driven reading programs, and mathematics drills. And the much discussed possibility of multiple assessments based on authentic tasks and developmental portfolios had been transformed into a centralized and overzealous standardized testing system. Not only had ideas associated with democratic classrooms faded from the scene, but now the politically naive standards-based reforms of the mainstream also had been overpowered by the new accountability movement of the archconservatives.

Almost everyone, including the most ardent advocates for democratic schools, would agree that there are certain things that young people ought to learn about in school. The real questions are these: What exactly is it that they are to learn? What form shall it take? And who gets to define those?

Democracy is dangerous to the power elite. Keep everybody scurrying to line up behind impossible standards, and nobody will have the energy to demand democracy.
Susan Ohanian, 2002

Early in the standards game, educators and politicians at the federal level and in most states reached a quick consensus that standards were to be based on the traditional academic subject areas. The political minefields of higher democratic purposes like cultural understanding, critical thinking, or problem solving had been amply revealed in the late 1980s when hard-line conservatives insisted that such "outcomes" violated their parental right to determine their children's values. For this reason, standards everywhere, and related standardized tests, have come to be focused almost exclusively on discipline-based academic content and skills. There are no "standards" for democratic living. Apparently, they do not matter. Apparently, it is acceptable to graduate students full of academics and bereft of democratic values.

Meanwhile, many educators and parents believe that if the curriculum is defined by subject-based content and skills, then the only appropriate way to "deliver" them to young people is through methods they generally associate with that kind of schooling: a subject-centered curriculum emphasizing direct instruction, substantial drill, assembly-line worksheets, frequent hard-nosed testing, and other sad relics of our nation's checkered educational history. Painful as that package of methods might have been in their own school days, many parents seem to have a kind of nostalgia for it, imagining that it somehow "built character" and wishing to have children share in their own bittersweet memories of boredom and irrelevance.

This longing for the past has been particularly prominent among upper-middle-class baby boomers who want their children to have an advantage over other children and have the money to try to make it happen. Not surprisingly, then, out of their nostalgia and fears have come not only the mournful call for a return to a classical curriculum, but also a veritable industry of educational media: books that tell us what cultural facts our children should know at every grade level, books and tapes retelling old fables that supposedly make children virtuous, and websites with ready-made lesson plans for parents. After all, the curriculum they seem to want is basically the same classical version as the one that dominated schools when the baby boomers were young. And, as Alfie Kohn (1998) has pointed out, the desire to maintain or regain that cultural and economic power is far stronger than the democratic imperative that other cultures and economic classes have a place in the curriculum as well. In another time and place, the push for a more inclusive curriculum might have some sway, but when the cultural interests of the academic elite converge with desires of conservative politicians and business leaders, there is not much space left for the democratic way.

Moreover, it is becoming increasingly clear that the idea of standards is leading inexorably toward standardization. This has mostly meant more and more standardized tests. But in a growing number of school districts, it also involves standardizing teaching methods as well as the scope and sequence of content and skills. In some places, teachers are given binders filled with scripted and sequenced lessons they are to follow. In funding reading initiatives, federal authorities spread their spoils only among schools that favor a phonics-based approach. And in district after district, teachers are told to standardize the sequence of unit topics by grade level and adopt standardized commercial curriculum kits to ensure that all children are taught the same things in the same way. Clearly, the belief that the standards movement would not dictate methods is turning out to be one more example of the naiveté of mainstream educators who are betrayed by the conservative politicians and policy makers Susan Ohanian (2002) calls the "Standardistas."

Why are our public schools going in this direction? To answer this question, more educators need to think about why they feel uncomfortable with the new accountability movement. Supposedly, the standards movement so many of them supported wasn't going to turn out this way. Standards were supposed to be broad and involve thinking and application, not just longer lists of facts and skills. Assessments were supposed to be multiple, authentic, and mostly local, not standardized and high-stakes. Teachers were supposed to have wide latitude in determining methods, not get prescriptive orders for sequencing content and test-prepping students. The push for standards was supposed to promote equity in achievement across race and class lines, not heighten desperation among our least privileged citizens. And that push was to have strengthened our public schools, not helped to punish and dismantle them.

Vivid contradictions like these should help all but the most naive to understand that the current momentum of the standards and testing movement has little to do with equity and achievement and everything to do with centralizing control over the curriculum. If it seems like there is less room for local educators to make curriculum decisions, if there seems to be more stress among educators, if it feels like teaching has lost its moral meaning, if it feels like there are more mandates and fewer resources, if it feels like poor and minority students are losing ground, if it feels like the school is becoming a corporate hierarchy, if teachers are more and more afraid to try out new ideas or fearful of making mistakes, if it is getting harder and harder to explain to students why certain things are included in the curriculum, if it feels like we are breaking faith with the democratic purposes of education like thinking and valuing—then welcome to the brave new world where the new accountability movement is taking us, whether we want to go or not.

> *The ideological effects of this position (vouchers and choice plans) are momentous. Rather than democracy being a political concept, it is transformed into a wholly economic concept.*
> Michael Apple, 2001

Beyond this, though, is a much more sinister intent. Our public schools are now in the midst of what seems like a death struggle to meet the requirements of what may go down as the most mean-spirited and antidemocratic law in education history, the one known popularly as No Child Left Behind. To comply with the law, schools must meet accelerating achievement standards that in the end require that all students everywhere, regardless of circumstances, score at the proficient level on federally approved standardized tests. While the law has been critiqued from many angles, the bottom line is that its requirements are impossible to meet. So there must be some larger purpose behind it. And there is. Insisting on impossible standards dooms the public schools to failure beyond their control. And if schools do not meet even one of the myriad mandates of the law, parents and students may eventually seek other school alternatives at taxpayer expense. This, in turn, clears the way for all kinds of for-profit, private education ventures supported mainly by public funds. Already there are many cases where for-profit companies manage public schools, and there are more subtle signs of what lies ahead for the prospects for truly democratic schools.

From "We" to "Me"

Perhaps I should not have been surprised on the day I dialed the main number for a public school district office and the person who answered cheerily announced, "Good morning, customer service." "Is this the school district?" I asked. "Yes, it is," the voice replied. I hung up without speaking, the purpose of the call forgotten. How could this be? Why would a school district have its phones answered "customer service"? Just to be sure, I tried the number again. Same voice, same greeting: "customer service."

> *A school system in which students must come together with others who are different may or may not further anyone's individual family goals, but it holds the potential to further our common goals as a democratic society.*
> Deborah Meier, 1995

Thinking back, I really should not have been surprised by that phone call. After all, we are living in an era when the role and purpose of all public institutions are being fundamentally redefined. I have lived my personal and professional life thinking that public institutions in a democratic society are meant to promote and support the public good. They may serve individual self-interest at the same time, but schools are *social* institutions, and their primary purpose is *social*. That would make my role, as citizen, a participant in its programs, a sometimes critic of its policies, a supporter of its social purposes, a volunteer in its cause, and more. Sure, the checkbook comes out every year to pay taxes. Citizens do have an obligation to support our public institutions. But we're paying toward the public good, singular, not for some private "goods."

And the public good is not just my good. It's the good of "we," not "me." Call me anything else, but don't call me "customer."

As free-market economies are glorified and public services privatized, the meaning of democracy is evolving almost exclusively as a matter of personal choice and self-interest, shrinking as it does the complementary notion of a public or common good (Apple and Beane 1995; Sehr 1997). Public conversation about the welfare of others is interrupted by a self-centered voice saying, "Enough about them, now let's talk about me." A vibrant, just, and ethical democracy involves the interests of individuals and the interests of the common good and the possibility that the two can be integrated— or at least kept in reasonable balance. When one begins to overwhelm the other, democracy shrinks, just as it is doing now when the crucial question seems to be, "What's in it for me?"

The public schools have been a widely publicized target of privatization, but they are not the only one. Shrinking financial support along with increasing control has diminished public libraries, media, museums, and parks. That any of these public venues, including schools, should only survive by selling itself and its naming rights to the highest bidder is simply astonishing in a society that brags that it is a democracy. But there it is. Right before our very eyes. The prospects for teaching the democratic way are being threatened not only by the new accountability movement within education but also by the larger move away from anything that smacks of democracy and the common good.

> *What we have in mind is education that develops in humans the disposition to make choices that benefit self and community mutually.*
> John Goodlad, 1997

Discouraging as this scenario may be, it must not lead to hopeless despair. Even as the forces opposed to democracy continue to ascend, many advocates for the democratic way seem to be finding their voice. Books, journal articles, websites, and other media have begun to use the "d" word again and in doing so to imagine a time when it will come back into fashion. It may even be that in defending the democratic way, its advocates will emerge with more clarity about its meaning. The road back may be long and difficult, but it can be traveled. If those who would diminish the democratic way can build such a powerful movement, why can't its advocates do the same?

On the Road Back

I have tried to do several things in this book. One, obviously, is to make a case for teaching the democratic way. Another is to explain what that means not only as a concept but also in terms of practical matters of curriculum, teaching, classroom community, and so on. Yet another is to invite teachers into the idea by showing how things already underway in their classrooms might be taken to a new level by thinking the democratic way and how there are many ways of bringing democracy to life. And I have tried to affirm the democratic ways of those teachers already well down the road. Looking back, there are several key ideas we need to keep in mind no matter how we move toward the democratic way. They are these.

If You Want Democracy, You Have to Be Democratic. The idea that schools should teach the democratic way of life is so cliché that even beginning teacher education students know to express it when they write the obligatory essay on "My Philosophy of Education." Yet all around us there are signs that people are confused or uninformed about democratic living. We are reluctant to voice dissent, we accept media information with little question, we excuse government malfeasance with a shrug, and we stand silently by while other people make decisions about our social and economic lives. How can we explain the dramatic disconnect between what our schools are supposed to teach and what we see in the behavior of so many people who went through those schools?

One popular way of explaining the disconnect is to say that the schools just aren't that powerful, that other social and political forces are much more influential. Maybe so. But it's hard to believe that the seventeen or eighteen thousand hours most people spend in schools comes to nothing in the end. After all, there are lots of things that people who attended schools seem to know. Why not the democratic way?

A more plausible explanation is that no matter how much they talk about it, schools don't really teach the democratic way of life. Mostly they just teach about it. Or more accurately, they teach about its symbols and structural procedures. We all learned something about the Declaration of Independence and the Constitution, even to the point of memorizing parts. We were told about the branches of government and sometimes about how a bill does or doesn't become a law. Sometimes, not always, we heard about political campaigns and elections if there happened to be an important one during a year we were taking history. But the methods used to teach in most schools lean heavily on the teacher as the sole authority for decisions; the textbook as the sole authority on information; the administration as the sole authority on governance; and the schedulers as the sole authority on time, space, and social connections.

It is little wonder that the potential link between schools and a democratic society can be dismissed so easily. Hearing about the structural procedures and symbols of a democratic government or about an election just won't get us democracy. Nor will the occasional discussion of some current issue so hot it can't be ignored. Nor will a yearly student council election. Critical thinking is learned only by thinking critically, reflection by reflecting, collaboration by collaborating, independence by working independently, social action by acting on social issues, compassion by caring for others, responsibility by having authentic and meaningful responsibilities, and decision making by making decisions.

The only way we can have democracy is by being democratic. If the school is to meet its obligation to teach the democratic way, then young people must live the democratic way inside it. And the only way that will happen is if the adults in the school make a conscious decision to bring democracy to life in their classrooms.

Democracy Is Not Just a Process; It Is About Something. Most efforts to promote democracy in classrooms and schools focus on promoting student participation in decision making. This makes good sense, since having a say in decisions that affect us is a key feature of democracy. Yet students have been excluded from almost every kind of decision making in schools. And where they have been involved, through student councils and the like, the issues they get to decide are mostly about social events and money-raising schemes. But even at its best, participation in decision making is only one aspect of a democratic culture, for democracy is not just a process. It is also about something.

At its core, democracy rests on three fundamental principles: respect for human dignity, concern for the common good, and faith that human beings working collaboratively are capable of resolving the issues that confront them. Living up to those three principles requires a commitment to other concepts, such as freedom, equity, and justice. For this reason, democratic schools and classrooms must involve more than just participatory processes. People in schools must be able to explore a wide range of information and viewpoints. They must be free to express ideas and values. All young people must have equitable access to the best opportunities and outcomes that the schools have to offer. They must have ample opportunities to work together in diverse groups on projects and other activities. They must be able to discuss and debate ideas.

> *A proper curriculum for democracy requires both the study of democracy and the practice of democracy.*
> Walter Parker, 2005

The principles and values of democratic living allow people to come together to name and work on significant issues that face them rather than being forced to live entirely according to the concerns and decisions of others. Collaborative work on pressing issues is a hallmark of the democratic way. This aspect of democracy requires that the school curriculum focus significant attention on compelling personal and social issues. It also requires that knowledge from the standard disciplines, popular culture, and other sources be brought together so that work on issues can be as well informed as possible. In a democratic culture, memorizing content from separate subject areas and thinking only within them simply will not do. Maybe the arrangement of knowledge into separate subjects was good enough for the Middle Ages, when the separate disciplines emerged among scholars. But it will hardly do in a complex world, where no single discipline or subject is sufficient to resolve any social issue of significance. Maybe participation in planning and decision making is a good place to start in creating more democratic schools. But if the curriculum avoids compelling personal and social issues, the work is only partly finished. Having a say without working on important issues creates only the illusion of democracy.

Democracy Is Not "Out There" Waiting for Us to Get There; It Is in the Here and Now. While democracy is definitely about something, that something is defined in terms of principles, values, and concepts. These are, in a sense, guidelines for how we will live and learn and work together democratically. But they are a compass, not a recipe. Equity, for example, means that what we do in our relations with others is done with an eye to fairness and that we take into account what people need, what resources they already have, and whether unfair obstacles have been placed in their path. This definition does not tell us exactly how to organize curriculum opportunities, how to group students, or how assessments should be constructed. What tips our thinking toward democracy is thinking about equity when we do decide how those things are done. Experience tells us that things look different when we think about equity.

Democracy would be a lot less complicated if such choices were sharply defined as part of the overall concept. Because they are not, figuring them out is itself a large part of democracy. Another large part of democracy is understanding that there may be many different ways of achieving equity or any other democratic principle, not just one. Still another is understanding that no decision is etched in stone; deciding things the democratic way involves continuous reflection, debate, and revision. The principles may be fairly well defined. How to move toward them is another matter.

These are extremely important ideas when thinking about teaching the democratic way. They remind us that democracy means figuring things out "on the ground." How will we live together in this classroom? What are some of the significant issues and topics we need to consider in the curriculum? How will we organize ourselves for projects? Questions like these are taken up by teachers and students when the classroom is a democratic community. True, there may be other forces at work in decisions, like state standards and general school behavior policies, but the final form ought to be shaped inside the classroom, not outside.

The "ground level" idea also means that teaching the democratic way cannot be lifted from another school or classroom. Teachers I know who plan integrative curriculum units with their students are often asked by other teachers for copies of their questions, activities, and resources. Their consistent reply is no. Embedded in their work is the democratic community and process out of which the units grow. Teachers who want such a curriculum for their own classrooms need to collaborate with their own students to create one. This is a hard pill for some teachers to swallow. Here are these purposeful, relevant, intellectually challenging, and engaging units, and they aren't for sale. They weren't found in a workbook or at an Internet site either. For the most part, those units and all they include are made within the classroom, sometimes "on the fly," but always with this year's group. Even when the theme was done last year and the year before that, the new group starts from scratch. They may have the same questions or use some of the same materials as last year's group. Or they may not.

Like democracy itself, democratic teaching and learning are not something "out there" waiting for us. They are created out of a democratic culture and community in the classroom. They are never settled; they are not a set of lesson plans to be used from year to year. Like democracy itself, they are created by a particular community in a particular place at a particular time. What happened last year is part of the resources and experience that the teacher brings to the classroom. But until this year's group arrives, the final form cannot be decided. After all, democracy is as much in the doing as in what is done. What democracy offers us is a compelling set of principles to guide us in the doing and in reflecting on what is done.

> *Democratic education is always purposeful but, moment by moment, not so predictable.*
> Carl Glickman, 2003

Democracy Is Messy. Classrooms where teachers and students plan together, where projects are almost always under way, where new questions and problems are constantly arising, and where small and large groups are frequently in discussion often seem noisy, cluttered, and even chaotic. Gone are the standardized lesson plans, the neat rows, the uncluttered desks, and the nicely filed worksheets. The reason, of course, is that democracy is a "messy" business compared to other approaches. It takes more time. It makes more noise. And it is full of surprises.

When we sincerely invite young people to participate in making plans or to push deeper into some inquiry, we never know for sure what may happen. Young people have lots of questions adults around them don't think of, sometimes because they see the world differently and sometimes because the adults have already addressed those questions in their own lives and are no longer puzzled by them. And one question or idea or discovery is almost certain to lead to another and then to another. In this respect, learning in a democratic classroom is more like following dirt roads than driving on superhighways. There is more to see but the road has more bumps and curves.

To make matters more difficult, the twists and turns of democratic teaching and learning are more complicated to explain than the linear and authoritarian methods of other approaches. Explaining to parents how a group arrives at decisions about classroom topics or activities is a lot more complex than showing them a textbook and a list of grading rules. Unfortunately, in a society that is used to getting its news in five sentences or less, any idea that takes time to explain is at risk. People who don't want democracy, or don't want it badly enough, typically say that it is slow and cumbersome compared to more authoritarian approaches. They are generally right about that. But even at its slowest and most cumbersome, it is still better in almost every way. And if we want democracy, do we have any other choice?

> *But democracy is and ever was messy, problematic, and it is always a work in progress.*
> Deborah Meier, 2004

Democracy Needs Protection. Teaching the democratic way takes us away from the linear, adult-dominated classroom. It involves a different way of thinking about young people, about relationships, about the curriculum, and about everything else that makes up life in schools. Such differences seem to bring out the most critical in people who prefer to have more control over what happens and less complexity in the curriculum. For this reason, teachers and other educators who use a democratic approach take a lot of abuse. How can one know when he or she is beginning to move in the democratic direction? When colleagues or parents start saying things like:

- "Children don't know what they need to learn, so don't ask them."
- "Children are too young to learn about things like that."
- "You waste too much time having discussions; you'll never get those students ready for the next year."
- "If you let students make decisions, they'll take over your classroom."
- "Children need to be told what to do."
- "Those kids need more structure."
- "The school shouldn't be involved in controversial issues."
- "Working in groups is holding back the smart kids."

These may seem like pretty harmless statements to anyone who has not been involved with democratic teaching and learning. But to those with experience, each one spells danger. Criticisms of collaborative learning have often led the way back toward ability grouping and tracking. Critics of using current issues in the curriculum have argued successfully for content standards and materials that avoid critical thinking. Those opposed to young people having a voice in curriculum decisions have often falsely, but successfully, claimed that democratic planning involves letting children do whatever they want.

Responding to such criticisms can sometimes open the door for clarifying conversations in schools where people are generally opposed or indifferent to democracy. Too often, though, the criticisms hide deeper agendas so tied up in self-interest that no amount of explaining will make a difference. Opposition to giving young people a voice sometimes masks a colleague's desire for control and authority in the classroom. Complaints about a lack of authoritarian methods might hide a deeper belief that some young people, usually those who are poor and of color, need tight control. Criticisms of collaborative learning are often heard from parents who are actually concerned that their children will somehow lose their competitive edge over peers. Agendas like these are hardly surprising in a society that has largely abandoned concern for the common good in favor of individual conquest.

For many educators who favor democratic approaches, the issue is not so much that they are unwilling to discuss their methods and the reasons behind them. It is that they are constantly on the defensive. Meanwhile, those who use authoritarian or self-interested methods seem rarely to be challenged. Since thoroughly democratic schools are rare, teachers who use democratic approaches are most often working as part of a small group or even alone. As criticisms come, one after another, they must constantly think about how and when to spend whatever "political capital" they have—what to compromise on, what to take a stand on. Sooner or later, they are worn down by the constant criticism. As more and more compromises are made, their work becomes "theoretically downsized." Eventually, they may leave or give up. It is an old story.

For this reason, democracy in schools, in whatever form it takes, needs constant protection. Almost always it is contradictory to the cultural norms of schools and society. Teachers and others who use democratic approaches desperately need administrative support to help deflect unfair criticism. But in the end, the only real protection for democratic education is democracy itself. Teachers who use democratic approaches must speak openly about what they do, take every opportunity to explain what they do and why, invite others to have conversations about curriculum and teaching, and continue to reflect carefully about the tensions and complexities of the democratic way. More than that, they must encourage their students to tell peers and parents about what and how they are learning. As teachers who use democratic approaches almost always come to understand, the further they push, the more able their students become in articulating the power of democratic living and learning. And while educational authorities seem to dismiss the views of teachers easily, they almost always find it hard to resist the voices of young people who value their educational experiences.

Democratic Teachers Need Friends and Support. Though I have mainly written this book for teachers, they are not the only educators who are interested in democratic teaching. Many school administrators and education professors have advocated loudly for the democratic way. Their arguments, especially those of university professors, have usually been extremely helpful. But sometimes, even though well intentioned, they get in the way. Particularly distracting is the tendency to always want something more from teachers, like a sharper political edge or more confrontational language and activities. Teachers work under difficult conditions—something that is easily forgotten by anyone who doesn't spend serious time in the schools. Working against the tide of the usual way and toward the democratic way is really hard. Often it proceeds in small steps. Educators outside the classroom need to celebrate those steps with teachers and not always immediately demand that they push further ahead before taking a breath. Moreover, "outsiders" need to be very careful not to imply that democratic teaching must always be confrontational. Teachers can make all kinds of moves toward the democratic way without necessarily coming into conflict with colleagues and administrators. Planning with students, using current social issues as a source of content and examples, encouraging student self-assessment, holding classroom meetings, and many other strategies can be used without permission, publicity, or confrontation.

Democratic teachers also need friends in the larger community if their work is to be sustained over time. Parents, guardians, and other community members who support the democratic way seem to make their presence and support known when teachers move in that direction. But others need to learn about the democratic way, especially those who have power in the community. It has often been the case that affluent, upwardly mobile parents have sought narrowly focused classical programs that they believe benefit their own children academically. I believe that they have been misinformed about that and misled by critics of the democratic way who play on parents' fears with dire predictions of academic and social disaster if children are taught that way. We need to show all parents how much more their children can learn and how much more committed they can be to learning when they have a say, when they are part of a vibrant community, when they are engaged in in-depth projects, when they have opportunities for reflection, and when they get to apply content and skills rather than just memorizing them. And we must be certain to get that message to the most powerful parents in the community. Why is this so important? Because word gets around. And if school district officials move to shut down democratic spaces, it is these parents who can exercise leverage with school boards and other officials to keep those spaces open.

As we communicate with groups outside the schools, we need to be very careful about language and focus. Parents, guardians, and other citizens are very interested in what and how much young people are learning. They are impressed with stories of students who are involved in community service projects and who create supportive communities within their schools. They also enjoy helping students with projects like oral histories. Not surprisingly, they are less interested in complicated theories of curriculum organization and blistering critiques of their schools. We need to give those outside the school lots of opportunities to know what young people are doing and learning about, especially by inviting them to help out in the school. And when we do get the chance to speak with them, we need to speak with hope for improving young people's lives rather than bitterness toward the

usual way of schooling. If they understand the first, they will figure out the second for themselves.

This is not to say that we should appear naively optimistic.
Harvey Kantor and Robert Lowe (2000) argue persuasively that one
of the reasons that progressive (and democratic) educators have
lost so much ground is that they stopped criticizing school bureau-
cracies in order to defend the schools against the wholesale attacks
of conservative critics. They have a point. I am certain that I am not
the only progressive who staunchly defended the schools against
attack knowing full well that some of the criticisms were accurate,
but was even more afraid of giving ground. We do not need to
diminish the democratic purposes and accomplishments of schools
when admitting that they also suffer from many inequities, cumbersome bureaucracy, and sometimes poor teaching. Moreover, by
admitting these things, we strengthen our position for what can be
defended. We also do not appear to have our heads in the sand.

At the End of the Day

Anyone who has not noticed the rise of profoundly conservative
and self-interested forces in education over the past decade or two
must surely have been in a deep and undisturbed sleep. These are
hard times for the democratic way and its advocates. One after
another, democratic programs and spaces in schools have been shut
down. In their place have come a steady stream of undemocratic
initiatives: boutique schools at the expense of a common, general
education and draconian standards; standardized tests; and standardized curriculum packages in place of the many creative and
successful programs built locally by teachers and students.

In the face of these movements, it is especially important to
remember that democracy has historically shown itself to be
extremely resilient. Its appeal is its optimistic and respectful view
of people at their best. They cannot be fooled forever and will
eventually see through the downsizing of their rights and opportunities. That is the democratic faith in human intelligence. Depress-
ing as the current state of education policy and politics may be, we
simply cannot forget to speak the language of possibility and the
politics of hope. Myles Horton, founder of the Highlander School,

at which the civil rights and other important democratic movements were partly launched, recognized the challenge of times
like ours:

> There are times when you can't go ahead. It's not within your
> power to deal with it, because the forces out there are such that
> you can't. You're not superhuman, and it's beyond your power.
> That's the time to hole up and start thinking. You watch the
> wind, and wait for it to blow your way. (1990, 200)

The large-scale push for teaching the democratic way has
reached such a moment. We do need to do some serious thinking
about what it means to teach that way and how we can do it and
sustain it better than before. But I also believe that the wind is
slowly beginning to blow our way. More and more authors and
speakers are using the "d" word again. Many mainstream educators are beginning to realize what they have lost and will continue
to lose under emerging education policies. At some point, the tide
will begin to turn, and in the search for something better, they
will discover the possibility of reclaiming the democratic purposes
of education.

6 Reclaiming the Democratic Way

There is certainly no shortage of those who criticize teaching the democratic way. I do not want to be unkind to them. In a democracy, they, too, are entitled to their views. But so many of their arguments simply baffle me. Some say that such teaching depends too much on whether the teacher is "good." But is there any approach that can be done well with bad teaching? Why pick on this one? Other critics say that teaching the democratic way isn't "academic" enough. Yet how can the significant work of democratic classrooms be done without what is usually called "academic" content and skills? And if those skills and content are such that they cannot be connected to learning the democratic way, are we then to graduate young people with their heads full of content and no social conscience? Still other critics simply do not believe that young people are capable of rising to the intellectual and social demands of democratic learning. Is our talk about high expectations for young people just so much lip service? If we think they cannot live the

While schools are not the only places where democratic virtues should be nourished, they form one of the few experiences all Americans hold in common.
George Wood, 1992

democratic way, how high can our expectations really be? Or our respect for their dignity? Or for our own?

Behind these criticisms, I suspect that there is one crucial reason why many people, educators included, criticize and resist the idea of teaching the democratic way. They have never experienced it. Of course, we have all heard from teachers and parents who say they have tried it and it doesn't work. But when those parents and teachers describe what they experienced, the stories are usually about manipulated planning, trivial topics, and forced connections among abstract subjects. I feel bad for those teachers and parents. This is not just poor democratic teaching. This is plain poor teaching, in the same way that constant lecturing, worksheets, drill, memorization, and competitive classrooms constitute poor teaching all by themselves rather than being examples of poor academic subject teaching. How can people have the kind of democratic classroom experience I have described? I do not see any other way than for more and more teachers to work through the political and procedural barriers presented by the usual way and begin to move toward the democratic way.

Lost and Found

My work over the past four decades has been focused on teaching the democratic way. In particular, it has been a search for answers to two questions:

- What does a democratic curriculum look like?
- How can we help teachers create and sustain a democratic curriculum?

Living as we do now in the midst of a great push *against* democracy, those questions seem more urgent than ever.

The last paragraph from John Dewey's *A Common Faith* (1934), etched on his memorial stone in the garden beside the chapel at the University of Vermont, speaks of our moral obligation to democracy:

> We who now live are parts of a humanity that extends into the remote past, a humanity that has interacted with nature. The things in civilization we most prize are not of ourselves. They

exist by grace of the doings and sufferings of the continuous human community in which we are a link. Ours is the responsibility of conserving, transmitting, rectifying and expanding the heritage of values we have received that those who come after us may receive it more solid and secure, more widely accessible and more generously shared than we have received it. (87)

Dewey wrote those words eight decades ago in the midst of a progressive movement in schools. Today, many critics dismiss the sentiments he and others so eloquently expressed, arguing that they were believed by few people and were mostly just slogans for a romantic and misguided emphasis on young people's experiences and concerns in the educational process. But I believe differently. Though they wrote long ago and their ideas were doomed by the greed of the economically powerful and the despicable repression of the McCarthy era, I believe that Dewey and other progressives of that earlier era spoke to the possibility of a deep and persistent commitment. That commitment was to the firm conviction that democracy is possible; that the democratic way of life can be lived; and that our schools should and can bring democracy to life in the curriculum, in school governance, in relations with the community, and in the hearts and minds of young people. That idea of democracy was not an empty shell, nor was it based on the vulgar notion of a free marketplace of competing alternatives from which people choose whatever suits their self-interests and their bank accounts.

Instead, democracy was to involve intelligent, well-informed, and collaborative participation in society. Creative individuality was to be balanced with concern for the welfare of others and a desire for a common good. Human dignity, equity, justice, and caring were to serve as both ends and means in our political, economic, and social relations. Out of these values a number of ideas emerged: democratic schools, intercultural education, problem-centered core programs, group learning, and more. Various curriculum designs surfaced as well, including sophisticated versions of what we still call curriculum integration (Beane 1997; Vars 1991). Accounts of practices like these and the urge for democracy that drove them are not fiction. Rather they are stories of a great tradition.

Moreover, to dismiss the historical fact of that democratic impulse, I would have to dismiss my own experience. My mother was herself a progressive teacher, by her own proud assertion, in the 1920s and 1930s. I grew up under her guidance and know what she thought the curriculum should be because I heard her tell various officials in our school and town. Years later, when I began writing about curriculum, her friends joked that I had learned my ideas before I ever left home and could have saved the tuition.

I would also have to forget my first years of teaching when I came into contact with some of those "old" progressives, speaking with them personally and also hearing them ferociously argue their democratic philosophy at professional conferences. We talked about the rights of young people, about democratic classrooms, about how students could help plan the curriculum, about how we could give social issues a larger place in the curriculum, about the unfairness of standardized tests, and about the despicable injustices in the larger society that crushed the souls of children. We were not afraid. We were part of a long line of progressive work. It was a different time in so many ways. And so much has been forgotten.

Knowing there is a history behind the democratic way is especially important today because now the talk about teaching and

Significant self and social themes guide the democratic curriculum.

learning is about something else entirely. We may want to wish otherwise, but it cannot be denied. The standards movement is in full swing, as are the pitiless testing schemes and standardized curriculum packages to go along with them. The long list of facts and skills they entail are called a "curriculum," and the definition of curriculum planning itself is reduced to the managerial function of aligning standards, overbearing tests, scripted lesson plans, and all the rest of the authoritarian mechanisms needed to control young people and their teachers. We are led to worship test scores, the false idols of education. And while the metaphorical bar has been raised for our children, politicians have explicitly refused to ensure that every school, and therefore every child, will have equitable resources to accomplish the standards.

> *The schools can teach democracy only as they become a democracy operating on, with, by, or through the beliefs which are basic to democratic living.*
> L. Thomas Hopkins, 1941

Schools are becoming simply one more example of niche products in a free marketplace of educational possibilities, where parents and others in the community are "consumers" of our teaching and our teaching a "product" for their consumerism. We make new programs for the affluent that will reaffirm their cultural dominance and separate their children from those who are nonprivileged. We make new programs for parents who wish to hide from their children's view those who do not subscribe to their own beliefs. We make new programs to satisfy the labor needs of greedy corporations. In short, we act as if the schools are maintained merely to serve the self-interests of the most powerful and vocal. Any obligation to a common good is dismissed here just as it is everywhere else in our society. We have become a profession of latest fads and glitzy programs with no pedagogical or moral compass to guide us, unless, of course, we mistake the bag of self-righteous virtues typically called "character education" for a moral philosophy.

I imagine myself a historian a century from now, looking back and wondering if people in our time actually believed that such an educational agenda met our "responsibility of conserving, transmitting, rectifying and expanding the heritage of values we have received that those who come after us may receive it more solid and secure, more widely accessible and more generously shared than we have received it." I would have expected something better of us than what is happening in this time.

> *If the schools of a democratic society do not exist for and work for the support and extension of democracy, then they are either socially useless or socially dangerous. At the best they will educate people who will go their way and earn their living indifferent to the obligations of citizenship in particular and of the democratic way of life in general. . . . But quite likely they will educate people to be enemies of democracy—people who will fall prey to demagogues, and who back movements and rally round leaders hostile to the democratic way of life.*
> James Mursell, 1955

And if I am wondering these things, imagine the hurt and anger so many teachers feel as they are blamed for so many problems in our schools when, in fact, the real source lies in the systematic purging of our moral and pedagogical infrastructure that has come from the movement to turn our schools and all other public institutions over to private greed and political self-interest. Our teachers should not be at the center of our scrutiny. Instead we must turn our attention to the conditions under which they are made to teach—the increasing stranglehold of authoritarian control, the insidious game of test score competition among unwitting students of different countries, the refusal to level the playing field of school resources, and the general failure of nerve in our society's social conscience. It is true that those conditions arise from movements outside the school and that we must resist them there. But it is just as true that they have invaded the curriculum of our schools.

I believe that it is time to reclaim the democratic purpose in education that is forged from the generous and noble aspirations of democracy and the democratic way of life. We cannot stand by and accept the pitiless curriculum increasingly forced on us as something worthy of our heritage or our young people's future. We should begin now to ask something else of the curriculum, something more than and quite different from what too many people are now asking.

We should ask that the curriculum bring diverse groups of young people together in communities of learning where they can live and work together in democratic ways, where their diversity is a prized aspect of the group rather than a criterion for the sort-

and-select machine. We should ask that the curriculum focus on topics and issues that are of real personal and social significance to both young people and the larger society. Justification for what the curriculum involves should be apparent and clear to everyone, especially students. The curriculum should never insult their intelligence or their capacity to recognize the irrelevant when they see it. We should ask that the curriculum treat young people with dignity, as real people who live in the real world and care about its condition and fate. We should ask that the curriculum value the knowledge and experience that young people bring with them to school, as well as the knowledge that they think would be worth pursuing. There should be room for them to have a say about their own learning experiences, and their say should really count for something.

We should ask that the curriculum engage important knowledge from many sources and be organized so that it is meaningful and accessible to young people. The rhythms and patterns of their inquiring young minds ought to be more important in determining the scope and sequence of knowledge than the recommendations of academics or bureaucrats who never see them and to whom they are only anonymous statistics in official reports. We should ask that the curriculum draw knowledge from many sources in academic and popular culture and that it privilege no one source nor serve the exclusive interests of any particular class or culture. We should want a curriculum that involves knowledge that is as rich in its diversity as the society itself.

We should ask that the curriculum bring our young people into contact with the most important and current ideas through the best resources we can find. Our children have a right to be well informed, and we have an obligation to help them in that way. We should ask that the curriculum offer our young people a chance to critique existing knowledge and construct new meanings, accepting no "fact" as true simply because it appears in a book or on the Internet. We should ask that the curriculum offer something better than short-answer, standardized tests, for these cannot possibly reveal what students really know or what is really worth knowing. Nor can such tests inquire as to whether the students are really sure of the answer, whether it perhaps momentarily escaped their memory, or whether they could explain it better another way. We should ask that the goals and expectations of the curriculum be reasonable and achievable for all young people and that none of them be excluded from those goals for reasons having to do with their race, class, or gender.

We should ask that the curriculum be kind to young people, uplifting their hopes and their possibilities rather than discouraging their spirits and aspirations. We should ask that it bring them joy in new insights and exciting discoveries. The work they do should involve more making and doing, more building and creating, and less of the deadening drudgery that too many of our curriculum arrangements still call for. We should ask that the curriculum challenge our young people to imagine a better world and to try out ways of making it so. We should ask that it bring them justice and equity, that it help them to overcome the narrow prejudices still so evident in our society. We should ask that the curriculum serve the best interests of our young people and our democracy and not be implicated in the ambitions of politicians or the profit desires of the corporate marketplace. In our schools, where the young must come involuntarily, we ought to guarantee that what is sought after is truly for them and not for the self-interests of others. We should ask that the curriculum be better for our young people than it was for us. It should not simply be what we had in school, but what we wished we could have had or, without prejudice, should have had.

Now I know that to publicly ask for a curriculum like this in the politics of our time is to invite ridicule from almost every corner of the profession and community. It is too idealistic, some would say, for the hard contests of the global marketplace. It is too dangerous, some would say, to give our children ideas like that. It is too soft, some would say, wanting to give their own child an advantage over others. It is too ambiguous, some would say, for young people who should be told right or wrong answers. Others will ask: Will it give our businesses a competitive edge in the global economy? Will our students score as well as those of other countries on international comparison tests? Will they get into elite colleges and universities?

To ask for a progressive curriculum must seem simply like an open invitation for ridicule from conservative pundits and talk-show hosts. Perhaps so. But that must not matter, for those of us who are citizen-educators are responsible for watching over the nobler ends of education in our democracy. The very possibility of such a curriculum is our moral challenge. Ours is the obligation to remember those who struggled to make a progressive and democratic history. Ours is the obligation to recapture the possibilities of democratic teaching and learning. Ours is the obligation to help and support teachers who want to begin to teach the democratic way. And ours is the obligation to seek out those who never let go of that hope—the courageous teachers who are keeping the progressive, democratic dream alive in these difficult times. Our obligation is to ask how we can help sustain and expand their will and their efforts—and to ask how, in answer to Dewey's call, we can make the meaning of their work "more widely accessible and more generously shared than we have received it."

"We're Still Hanging On"

"We're still hanging on," George West tells me, "maybe not as democratic as we used to be, but we're still very student-centered." Twenty-five years later and several hundred miles away, I have called the Children's School in hopes of finding out whether the school whose story began this book has kept its very democratic character. One of the key teachers early on, Mr. West is now the principal. The weekly town meetings continue, but final decisions are more likely to be made by adults rather than by the old one-person, one-vote process. An exciting Activities Program, whose offerings are partly drawn from children's suggestions, has replaced the bicycle repair shop, the post office, lunchtime play productions, and other aspects of the old community. Most teachers still involve children in classroom planning in some way, but the curriculum is not so centered on real-life activities and issues. The report cards have moved from descriptive reporting to percentage grades in the intermediate levels, but are beginning to move back again. In an era when so many schools have retreated to a drill-and-worksheet regime, the Children's School is still a remarkable place in a lot of ways. As Mr. West puts it, "We had a lot more going for us so we fell back less than other places."

But time and politics have taken a toll on the school. Merging with another elementary school meant joining with another faculty who had not necessarily thought about democratic schools. With them came parents who wanted the usual kind of school to prevail in the merger. Commitment to the democratic way for a few faculty from the original Children's School drifted toward the usual way of doing things as well. Importantly, some key leaders moved on to other positions or places fairly early on. But George is hopeful. "I feel like the pendulum is starting to swing back again," he says.

Our talk about the school finished, we turned to the banter of long-ago friends: retirement plans, news of mutual acquaintances, and the vagaries of aging. Having said my thanks and ready to hang up, I was unprepared for what George said next: "I always think about that time and what it was like to be really progressive. Some of us still talk about it when we get together. We wonder how far we could have taken the idea of the community and how far we could have taken the idea of the curriculum emerging from the experiences of the students." As we said good-bye, he added, "We still remember, we're still hanging on."

What is it about teaching the democratic way that once people have really done it, they cannot get free of its pull? Several teachers who created the integrative and democratic curriculum projects I mentioned in Chapter 2 have told me that they can never go back to what they call "the old way." A few who were ordered to do so actually left teaching rather than have their professional commitments diminished. My great colleague Smokey Daniels, who has had to watch the dismantling of several successful democratic school projects in urban elementary and high schools, insists that the experience of democratic teaching has a "transcendent power" that haunts those who have to give it up.

Students, too, when they have been in such spaces, seem to carry their memory a long time after. A high school senior, asked to write her educational history for an advanced placement class, remembered the problem-centered, collaboratively planned themes in her seventh-grade class and wrote, "It was the only time I ever had to really think . . . it was the only time I was really challenged." Looking back on his time in an upper-elementary democratic classroom, a college student told me, "We were a community and we all learned to work with our classmates, even those we didn't like." Barbara Brodhagen (1995) tells of a follow-up interview with a group of students who had been with her and a teaching partner in a democratic classroom. After several had talked about how much they had learned, they were asked if they thought the school's computer had made their class a special grouping of students rather than the heterogeneous mix it was supposed to be. One student said simply, "We weren't a special group . . . but the situation made us special."

The writer John Parker tells about great athletes, years after leaving their games, who still hear what he calls the "roar that will never leave their heads." I think that is probably the same phenomenon those democratic educators and their former students talk about. Their recollections suggest that the pull of democracy is partly about the dignity they feel and also about a yearning for ways of doing things that are caring and ethical. In saying that, I don't mean to romanticize life inside democratic schools and classrooms. Creating them is very hard work and they are, by definition, "messy" places. But I really do believe that there is something extraordinarily powerful about the way they look and feel and sound.

Over many years, I have known and worked with some of the best (and best-known) democratic teachers around. Now, late in my career, I spend a lot of time in a school where some young teachers are hard at work toward teaching the democratic way. They seem drawn to this kind of work by a generous impulse toward their students and a genuine belief in the possibilities for learning the democratic way. In their classrooms, even after all these years, I still sometimes find myself emotionally overwhelmed by the sense of dignity and hope that the democratic way inspires. Dignity . . . and Hope. That is why, no matter how bleak the current situation seems, the democratic way will sooner or later find its way into the hearts and minds of more and more teachers, and into the culture and curriculum of their classrooms and schools. And from there into the lives of their students.

*A*ppendix: Reflecting on the Democratic Way of Teaching

Teachers who choose the democratic way constantly reflect on their work. Inquiring into things, including one's own practice, is a hallmark of democratic teaching and learning. Inside Chapter 1 and at the end of Chapters 2, 3, and 4, I listed some of the kinds of questions democratic teachers ask about teaching, curriculum, classroom culture, and school structures and policies. Those questions are gathered together in this appendix for easy reference. Gertrude Noar did the same thing in her wonderful 1963 book, *Teaching and Learning the Democratic Way.* Anyone who takes the time to find that book will see that teaching the democratic way has a long history, and the kinds of questions teachers would reflect upon today have been a part of that history all along.

Choosing the Democratic Way

- How do we think about young people in our school? Are they treated with dignity? Do we talk about them as people or simply as students? Do we speak of our relationship with young people in ways that suggest that school is "us versus them"?
- How does our teaching make use of democratic processes? Do young people have a say in what happens in our classrooms? How do they learn to work together? Are they active and inquiring or simply passive recipients of our words?
- Do the structures of our school treat young people in just and equitable ways? Do all students have access to rich and varied experiences? Do groupings mirror the diversity of the community? Do school outcomes suggest that no group

within the school has had a better chance at succeeding than any other? Is there evidence of equitable success among all groups and cultures in the school? Are the resources of the school equitably distributed across the whole school enrollment?

- Does the curriculum include space to learn about and work on personal and social issues inside and outside the school? Does the curriculum respect diverse cultures? Is diversity viewed as a problem to be overcome or as a positive aspect of the school that enriches the possibilities for living and learning?

- Do the adults in the school work as a democratic community? Do they work together on issues and problems? Do they collaborate on curriculum work? Do they reflect on their teaching individually and collaboratively?

- Is the school governed democratically? Do young people, faculty and staff, parents and guardians, and other community members have opportunities to participate in thinking about and making decisions regarding the school?

- Do school staff and policies treat students with dignity and respect? Are communications honest and open? Do all parents and guardians have equitable access to decision-making policies and procedures?

Teaching for Democracy's Sake

- Did my students have an adequate and appropriate voice in classroom planning?
- Was the content we focused on of some social significance?
- Were students involved in rigorous and authentic activity?
- Did we consult a variety of sources and viewpoints in our research?
- Did we critically examine information and viewpoints?
- How could our work extend more often into community service?
- Did we use a variety of ways to reflect on and evaluate our work and our group?
- Did students have an adequate and appropriate say in creating our evaluation?

- Did students have an adequate voice in evaluating their own work?
- Were my expectations high enough, and did I push all students to do well?
- Was there enough variety in activities and materials so that all students had an equitable chance to access the curriculum?
- Did I play out my role as teacher democratically?

Living the Democratic Way

- Do I see my classroom as a community or simply a collection of individuals? Do we work collaboratively? Do students participate in governing and maintaining the community?
- Do I see young people simply as students, or do I try to understand them as whole persons? Is their agenda evident in the agenda of the classroom? Do I take them seriously as people?
- Do I think of the diversity among students, as a problem to overcome or as an asset to the potential richness of the classroom community? Are varieties of cultures evident in the curriculum, the structures, and the aesthetics of our classroom? Does the particular culture to which I belong dominate the classroom, or is it one among many that are evident?
- Is our classroom a "court of knowledge"? Do we ask lots of questions about things? Do we search for explanations behind events, issues, and ideas? Do we access a wide variety of resources in search of wide-ranging opinions and ideas? Do we consider the ethics of situations, issues, and events?
- Am I considering only structures like grouping and governance in moving toward a democratic classroom, or am I also working toward a democratic curriculum?

Being a Democratic Teacher

- Who are we, and what do we believe about young people, our schools, our communities and cultures, and our obligations?

- Do we act in ways that invite other professionals to join us, or are we overly critical of colleagues?
- Do we always have to invent new ways to find community, or can we find within the schools already existing possibilities for doing so?
- If we are among those who supposedly "teach" teachers, can we say that we are really seeking to create more democratic spaces, or do we only talk about what teachers should do in their schools?

References

Allen, J., ed. 1999. *Class Actions: Teaching for Social Justice in Elementary and Middle School*. New York: Teachers College Press.

Apple, M. 1993. *Official Knowledge: Democratic Education in a Conservative Age*. New York and London: Routledge.

———. 2001. *Educating the "Right" Way*. New York: RoutledgeFalmer.

Apple, M. W., and J. A. Beane, eds. 1995. *Democratic Schools*. Alexandria, VA: Association for Supervision and Curriculum Development.

Bastian, A., N. Fruchter, M. Gittell, C. Greer, and K. Haskins. 1986. *Choosing Equality*. Philadelphia: Temple University Press.

Beane, J. 1990a. *Affect in the Curriculum: Toward Democracy, Dignity, and Diversity*. New York: Teachers College Press.

———. 1990b. *A Middle School Curriculum: From Rhetoric to Reality*. Columbus, OH: National Middle School Association.

———. 1997. *Curriculum Integration: Designing the Core of Democratic Education*. New York: Teachers College Press.

Beane, J., B. Brodhagen, and G. Weilbacher. 2005. "Show Me the Money." In H. Daniels and M. Bizar, *Teaching the Best Practice Way: Methods That Matter*. Portland, ME: Stenhouse 291–96.

Beyer, L. E., ed. 1996. *Creating Democratic Classrooms: The Struggle to Integrate Theory and Practice*. New York: Teachers College Press.

Bigelow, W., and R. Peterson, eds. 1991. *Rethinking Columbus*. Milwaukee, WI: Rethinking Schools Ltd.

Boomer, G., N. Lester, C. Onore, and J. Cook. 1992. *Negotiating the Curriculum*. London: Falmer.

Brady, M. 2000. "The Standards Juggernaut." *Phi Delta Kappan* 81(9): 652–56.

———. 2004. "Priceless Lesson: Teacher, Students Put Learning Into Action, Show What Can Be Done." *Orlando Sentinel*, 22 May, A19.

Brodhagen, B. 1994. "Assessing and Reporting Student Progress in an Integrative Curriculum." *Teaching and Change* 1: 238–54.

———. 1995. "The Situation Made Us Special." In M. W. Apple and J. A. Beane, eds., *Democratic Schools*. Alexandria, VA: Association for Supervision and Curriculum Development 83–100.

Brodhagen, B., G. Weilbacher, and J. Beane. 1998. "What We've Learned from 'Living in the Future.'" In L. Beyer and M. Apple, eds., *The Curriculum: Problems, Politics, and Possibilities*. Albany, NY: SUNY Press 117–33.

Carnegie Corporation and the Center for Information and Research on Civic Learning and Engagement. 2003. *The Civic Mission of Schools*. Available at www.civicmissionofschools.org/.

Cobb, C. 1991. "Mississippi Freedom School Curriculum—1964." *Radical Teacher* 40(1): 5–34.

Counts, G. 1952. *Education and American Civilization*. New York: Bureau of Publication, Teachers College, Columbia University.

Daniels, H., and M. Bizar. 1998. *Methods That Matter: Six Structures for Best Practice Classrooms*. York, ME: Stenhouse.

Daniels, H., M. Bizar, and S. Zemelman. 2001. *Rethinking High Schools*. Portsmouth, NH: Heinemann.

DePung, M. 2001. "The Genesis of a Teacher Study Group: Analysis and Implications for a Democratic School." *Democracy and Education* 14(2): 15–18.

Dewey, J. 1916. *Democracy and Education*. New York: Macmillan.

———. 1934. *A Common Faith*. New Haven, CT: Yale University Press.

———. 1938. *Experience and Education*. Bloomington, IN: Kappa Delta Pi.

————. 1946. *Problems of Men.* New York: Philosophical Library.

Faunce, R., and N. Bossing. 1951. *Developing the Core Curriculum.* New York: Prentice Hall.

Freire, P. 1970. *Pedagogy of the Oppressed.* Translated by M. Bergman. New York: Continuum.

Gay, G. 2003/2004. "The Importance of Multicultural Education." *Educational Leadership* 61(4): 30–35.

Gastil, 1993. *Democracy in Small Groups: Participation, Decision-Making, and Communications.* Philadelphia: New Society.

Glickman, C. 2003. *Holding Sacred Ground: Essays on Leadership, Courage, and Endurance in Our Schools.* San Francisco: Jossey-Bass.

Goodlad, J. 1997. *In Praise of Education.* New York: Teachers College Press.

Grady, E. 2003/2004. "Future Shock." *Educational Leadership* 61(4): 65–69.

Green, M. 1985. "The Role of Education in a Democracy." *Educational Horizons* 63: 3–9.

Gutmann, Amy. 1987. *Democratic Schools.* Princeton, NJ: Princeton University Press

Hall, I., C. Campbell, and E. Miech, eds. 1997. *Class Acts: Teachers Reflect on Their Own Classroom Practice.* Cambridge, MA: Harvard University Press.

Hargreaves, A., and M. Fullan. 1998. *What's Worth Fighting for Out There?* New York: Teachers College Press.

Hess, D. 2002. "Teaching Controversial Public Issues Discussions: Learning from Skilled Teachers." *Theory and Research in Social Education* 30(1): 10–41.

Hirsch, E. D. 1987. *Cultural Literacy.* Boston: Houghton Mifflin.

Hopkins, L. T. 1941. *Interaction: The Democratic Process.* New York: Heath.

Horton, M. 1990. *The Long Haul*. New York: Doubleday.

Hunt, J. 2001. "A Collective Progressive Voice in Special Education." *Democracy and Education* 14(1): 2.

Johnson, D., R. Johnson, E. Holubec, and P. Roy. 1991. *Cooperation in the Classroom*. Edina, MN: Interaction Books.

Kantor, H., and R. Lowe. 2000. "Bureaucracy Left and Right: Thinking About the One Best System." In L. Cuban and D. Shipps, eds., *Reconstructing the Common Good in Education*. Stanford, CA: Stanford University Press 130–47.

Kelley, E. 1962. *In Defense of Youth*. Englewood Cliffs, NJ: Prentice Hall.

Kohn, A. 1996. *Beyond Discipline: From Compliance to Community*. Alexandria, VA: Association for Supervision and Curriculum Development.

———. 1998. "Only for My Kid: How Privileged Parents Undermine School Reform." *Phi Delta Kappan* 79(8): 568–77.

Kozol, J. 1975. *The Night Is Dark and I Am Far from Home*. New York: Simon & Schuster.

La Escuela Fratney. 2003/2004. *Themes for La Escuela Fratney 2003–2004*. Available at www.milwaukee.k12.wi.us/pages/MPS/Schools/elem/fratney/Welcome/themes.

Lipka, R. 1997. "Research and Evaluation in Service Learning." In J. Schine, *Service Learning*, Ninety-Sixth Yearbook of the National Society for the Study of Education. Chicago: University of Chicago Press.

Lockwood, A. 1985/1986. "Keeping Them in the Courtyard." *Educational Leadership* 43: 9–10.

Lockwood, A., and D. Harris. 1985. *Reasoning with Democratic Values*. New York: Teachers College Press.

Loewen, J. 1995. *Lies My Teacher Told Me: Everything Your American Hostory Textboooks Got Wrong*. New York: Simon & Schuster.

Marks, H., F. Newmann, and A. Gamoran. 1996. "Does Authentic Pedagogy Increase Student Achievement?" In F. M. Newmann and Associates, *Authentic Achievement: Restructuring Schools for Intellectual Quality.* San Francisco: Jossey-Bass. 49–73.

McDermott, C., ed. 1998. *Beyond the Silence: Listening for Democracy.* Portsmouth, NH: Heinemann.

Meier, D. 1995. *The Power of Their Ideas: Lessons for America from a Small School in Harlem.* Boston: Beacon.

———. 2004. "NCLB and Democracy." In D. Meier and G. Wood, eds., *Many Children Left Behind: How the No Child Left Behind Act Is Damaging Our Children and Our Schools.* Boston: Beacon. 66–78.

Meier, D., and P. Schwartz. 1995. "Central Park East Secondary School: The Hard Part Is Making It Happen." In M.W. Apple and J. A. Beane, eds, *Democratic Schools.* Alexandria, VA: Association for Supervision and Curriculum Development 26–40.

Mikel, E. 2000. "Deliberating Democracy." In P. Joseph, S. Bravmann, M. Windschitl, E. Mikel, and N. Green, *Cultures of Curriculum.* Mahwah, NJ: Lawrence Erlbaum 115–36.

Mursell, J. 1955. *Principles of Democratic Education.* New York: Norton.

Nagel, N. 1996. *Learning Through Real-World Problem Solving.* Thousand Oaks, CA: Corwin.

National Association for Core Curriculum. 1985. *Core Today: Rationale and Implications.* 3rd ed. Kent, OH: The Association.

National Commission on Excellence in Education. 1983. *A Nation at Risk.* Washington, DC: U.S. Department of Education.

National Service Learning Clearinghouse. *What Is Service Learning?* Available at www.servicelearning.org/.

Nelson, J. R. with L. Frederick. 1994. "Can Children Design Curriculum?" *Educational Leadership* 51(5): 71–74.

Newmann, F., and Associates. 1996. *Authentic Achievement: Restructuring Schools for Intellectual Quality.* San Francisco: Jossey-Bass.

Noar, G. 1963. *Teaching and Learning the Democratic Way.* New York: Prentice-Hall.

Ogle, D. 1986. "K-W-L: A Teaching Model That Develops Active Reading of Expository Text." *Reading Teacher* 39: 564–70.

Ohanian. S. 2002. *What Happened to Recess and Why Are Our Chidren Struggling in Kindergarten?* New York: McGraw-Hill.

Palmer, P. 1998. *The Courage to Teach.* San Francisco: Jossey-Bass.

Parker, W. 2005. "Teaching Against Idiocy." *Phi Delta Kappan* 86(5): 344–51.

Peterson, B. 1995. "La Escuela Fratney: A Journey Toward Democracy." In M. Apple and J. Beane, eds., *Democratic Schools.* Alexandria, VA: Association for Supervision and Curriculum Development 58–82.

Ravitch, D. 2000. *Left Back: A Century of Failed School Reform.* New York: Simon & Schuster.

Rethinking Schools. 2004. *The New Teacher Handbook.* Milwaukee, WI: Rethinking Schools.

Rosenstock, L., and A. Steinberg. 1995. "Beyond the Shop: Reinventing Vocational Education." In M. Apple and J. Beane, eds., *Democratic Schools.* Alexandria, VA: Association for Supervision and Curriculum Development 41–57.

Santone, S. 2003/2004. "Education for Sustainability." *Educational Leadership* 61(4): 60–63.

Schubert, W. 1986. *Curriculum: Perspective, Paradigm, and Possibility.* New York: Macmillan.

Sehr, D. 1997. *Education for Public Democracy.* Albany: SUNY Press.

Shaw, C. C. 1993. "A Content Analysis of Teacher Talk During Middle School Team Meetings." *Research in Middle Level Education* 17(1): 27–45.

Soder, R., ed. 1996. *Democracy, Education, and the Schools.* San Francisco: Jossey-Bass.

Soder, R., J. Goodlad, and T. McMannon, eds. 2001. *Developing Democratic Character in the Young*. San Francisco: Jossey-Bass.

Thomas, J. 2000. *A Review of Research on Project-Based Learning*. Available at www.autodesk.com/foundation.

Vars, G. F. 1991. "Integrated Curriculum in Historical Perspective." *Educational Leadership* 49(1): 14–15.

Varvus, M. 2002. *Transforming the Multicultural Education of Teachers*. New York: Teachers College Press.

Wesley, C. 1941. "Education for Citizenship in a Democracy." *Journal of Negro Education* 10: 68–78.

Williams, R. 1961. *The Long Revolution*. London: Chatto and Windus.

Wineburg, S., and D. Martin. 2004. "Reading and Rewriting History." *Educational Leadership* 62(1): 42–45.

Wood, G. 1992. *Schools That Work*. New York: Dutton.

Zapf, R. 1959. *Democratic Processes in the Secondary Classroom*. Englewood Cliffs, NJ: Prentice Hall.

Zinn, H. 1980. *A People's History of the United States*. New York: Harper and Row.

$\mathcal{I}$ndex